Aug. 21, 1993

To Keith

— in appreciation

PARADOXES
in the
MODERN
FAMILY

Paradoxes
IN THE
Modern
Family

MILTON R. SAPIRSTEIN, M.D.

Gardner Press, Inc.

NEW YORK LONDON SYDNEY

Gardner Press, Inc.
19 Union Square West
New York, New York 10003

Library of Congress Cataloging-in-Publication Data

Sapirstein, Milton R., 1914-
    Paradoxes in the modern family/by Milton R. Sapirstein.
      p. cm.
    ISBN 0-89876-194-8
    1. Family—United States—Psychological aspects.
    2. Intergenerational relations—United States. I. Title.
HQ536.S333 1992
    646.7'8—dc20
                                     92-20716
                                       CIP

To My Family

ACKNOWLEDGMENTS

I would like to thank my sister, Pearl Whitman, Associate Professor Emeritus at the Mandel School of Applied Social Sciences, Case Western Reserve University, for reading the manuscript as the member of the family delegated to alert me to any possible unintended (or, perhaps, intended) personal references which might be inappropriate.

To my children and their families: Thank you for making me so proud of you. Without your achievements, this book would not have been possible—I could never have written it if I did not admire so much the results of your mother's nurturing and influence. While I was writing this book, I became less of a father and grandparent. You were very tolerant of this, and I trust it was worth it—it was for me. We live so long nowadays that it becomes necessary to take an occasional vacation from our accustomed roles.

My appreciation and thanks also to my publisher, Gardner Spungin, and to Maria Rodriquez Gil, my editor.

PREFACE

This book is a personal document. Having practiced psychiatry and psychoanalysis for over forty-five years and been a family man for a little longer, I've gleaned some insight into attitudes and other factors that contribute to dissension within the family, and would like to share my views and findings with the reader. The ideas and opinions I express are based on both my professional and personal experience, not formal studies. (However, since I rarely lose touch with my former patients, my statistical base is reasonably large.)

I started writing about changes within the modern family almost forty years ago with my book *Paradoxes of Everyday Life* (1953), in which I challenged the ridiculous standards of the day for normal sexual behavior, and questioned the rigidity of our conceptions of motherhood.

In the years since, feminism, the sexual revolution, the increasing life span, the escalating divorce rate, the breakdown of authority, the use of drugs—all these have caused family patterns to shift to the point of unrecognizability. Where are we going? And where have we been?

While attempting to shed light on general family problems, this book makes no attempt to be all-encompassing. Each chapter consists of thoughts and insights on a particular aspect of family life; where I have no contribution to make, nothing is said.

Since this book reflects my personal opinions on the family, it may not cover all points of view. While trying hard to be fair minded, it is always difficult to let go of certain prejudices and convictions that have been a part of one's makeup for many years. Still, I hope that my observations on the family today will be helpful to readers into the 1990s.

INTRODUCTION

The Family Today

We are coming to the end of the twentieth century. People today are living longer, and more than twenty years have passed since the women's and youth movements of the 1960s, both of which significantly contributed to the dismantling of the traditional family unit as we once knew it.

My generation has had some unique experiences that are worth reviewing and that may shed some light on these issues. With few precedents to guide us, we survived the Great Depression, World War II, and all of the social upheavals of the past thirty years. We have witnessed a sexual revolution that has brought about an escalating divorce rate, contraception as the rule of the day, widespread availability of legal abortions, and delays in marriage and pregnancy. This, along with the rebellions of the 1960s and the almost universal breakdown of authority, has produced a previously inconceivable chaos in society at large and precipitated dramatic changes in our conception of what constitutes a family, as experienced, for example, by working mothers and single parents.

This is a book about families growing older, about the often complicated relationships between parents and children when the children are adults and childhood games are presumably long gone. It's a book about how increasing survival rates, the lessening of personal commitments, the erosion of the principles of the Fifth Commandment, and the growing self-preoccupation of many people have changed the family and created complex problems for its members. Some of the questions this book will attempt to answer include the following:

How do we cope with parent-child relationships when the child is no longer a child and, in fact, may be a parent or grandparent? When do parents stop being responsible for their adult children, especially now that the senior generation is more prosperous than its offspring? Since the state took over much of the responsibility of caring for our aged with the passing of the Social Security Act in the 1930s and, more recently, the establishment of Supplemental Security Income (SSI) and of Medicaid, is it ever acceptable for a child to walk away from the responsibilities to his elderly parents? How do we deal with grandchildren when they become adults and stop adoring us? How can we maintain strong family relationships when one of the parents dies prematurely? Now that people are living longer and it's more acceptable for widowed parents to take on new partners, how does a parent deal fairly with his children's concerns when he decides to remarry? What role do factors such as money, the reversal of gender roles, loneliness, courage, fear of death, and social status play in the family today?

Unfortunately, most people do not want to discuss these issues. Many of my friends have horrendous problems with their grown children (and vice versa) which both sides seem embarrassed to talk about. It's almost as if parent-child problems should not exist once the children are past adolescence. Yet we know from experience that parent-child patterns may persist throughout our lifetimes, especially if we refuse to look at them.

I hope that the chapters that follow—each a personal reflection on a family-related topic—will provide some useful ideas to help the reader find constructive ways of coping with the complex problems faced by the family today.

CONTENTS

ABOUT THE AUTHOR

MILTON R. SAPIRSTEIN was born on November 30, 1914. He has been a physician for more than fifty years, and has practiced psychoanalysis for over forty-five years. He is an Accredited Psychiatrist and Neurologist of the American Board of Psychiatry and Neurology and is presently Emeritus Professor of Clinical Psychiatry at The Mount Sinai Hospital in New York City.

A graduate of the College of the City of New York and of The New York University School of Medicine, Dr. Sapirstein has been on the staff at Montefiore Hospital, Psychiatric Institute, Hillside Hospital, Bronx Veterans Hospital, and Mount Sinai Hospital. In addition, he taught or did research at four medical schools: N.Y.U. School of Medicine (pharmacology), Yale University School of Medicine (physiology), College of Physicians and Surgeons of Columbia, (psychiatry), and Mount Sinai School of Medicine (neurology and psychiatry).

Dr. Sapirstein is the author of two books, *Emotional Security* (1948) and *Paradoxes of Everyday Life* (1953), and has an extensive scientific bibliography. He lectured widely on popular psychiatric subjects in the 1940s and 1950s at the Ethical Culture Society, Free Synagogue, Cooper Union, and other popular educational forums, but retired from the world of popular psychiatric writing and lecturing due to concerns about the intrusion of his growing notoriety into his professional activities and family life.

Dr. Sapirstein received his credentials in psychoanalysis from Columbia University, where he was appointed a training analyst at the age of thirty-four. He is a member of the American Psychoanalytic Association, and is still in full-time practice in New York City. Married for forty-five years, he is widowed, is the father of two sons, and has four grandchildren.

CHAPTER 1

THE DECLINE OF AUTHORITY

Who Killed the Fifth Commandment?

*T*he biblical basis for a parent's authority over a child is found in the Fifth Commandment: "Honor thy father and thy mother: that thy days may be long upon the land which the Lord thy God giveth thee." This commandment says nothing about love—only honor—with a long life being our only reward.

But a questioning of, and revolt against, parental and all other forms of authority has taken place in our society in the past thirty or so years, dramatically altering the structure of the family unit and creating a great rift between the generations. While this erosion of the Fifth Commandment principles reached its peak during the 1960s and 1970s, its seeds had been sown much earlier than that.

I believe that this breakdown of authority is basically the result of the emergence, during the 1920s and 1930s, of the world-power dictatorships. Stalin, Hitler, Mussolini—all three simultaneously attacked the authority of the family and of religion. This double-pronged attack on traditional values had never been tried before. Old monarchies had maintained their authority by strongly supporting both religion and the family. Not so for twentieth-century dictators, who deposed both God and father at the same time. They wanted those roles for themselves—to become God and father to their people, and rule the world absolutely. But their power had been illegally seized, not delegated to them by traditional procedures. Thus, in establishing and enforcing their iron rule, they destroyed the fabric of their societies. In 1923, Lenin said, "We must hate—hatred is the basis of Communism. Children must be taught to hate their parents if they are not Communists." The results of this doctrine were both shocking and heartbreaking: In 1932, Pavlik Morovov, who was then thirteen years old, denounced his father as a class enemy; Pavlik himself was subsequently murdered as an informer. Both Lenin and Stalin established programs to undermine the concepts of traditional religion and to encourage youth to ignore their parents.

During the 1930s, the Russian experiment profoundly influenced the intellectuals of the West, who set out to spread the new gospel through books and magazines. These new ideas, when combined with the concepts of progressive education and the discoveries being made by psychoanalysis, made many parents unsure about their own judgments, way of thinking, and right to impose their values on their children. Thus, with no respect for parents or religion to fall back on, traditional authority began to collapse. There was no longer any hope to be found in the concept of Heaven, and very little you could count on here on earth.

But it was during the 1960s, and part of the 1970s, that the revolt against parental authority manifested itself most strongly—the older generation was no longer in charge; our children were no longer willing to listen to anyone over thirty.

The youth and women's rebellions permanently altered the structure of both the family and society at large. The political aftereffects of these rebellions are still powerfully obvious. And, in the schools, the discarding of our old reliance on and respect for authority was expressed by a patient of mine who was a teacher in a ghetto school: "We always experienced a lot of defiance from the children in the classroom. But it's different now. When I give an order, nobody even gets defiant; they just don't pay any attention to me. They don't even listen. It's as if they don't recognize the fact that authority exists at all!'' Within the family, the result was also quite clear: peer pressure replaced parental authority, causing rudeness to replace respect and equality to be expressed with increasing vulgarity: "Let it all hang out, man!'' Traditional conventions of manners and dress were discarded as elitist, and old symbols of authority like the flag are treated disrespectfully even today.

These changes in attitudes and values are by no means confined to the American family; they are world-wide, evident in Europe, Russia, China, and as prevalent in South America as in Southern California. This pandemic of rebellion against old values pits the young against the old everywhere.

But the results of this erosion of trust and respect for the older generation, which made family authority and wisdom obsolete, are not always positive ones for the generation of young rebels, who end up losing the support of the families they've rejected.

At one time, the personal difficulty of a younger person was a family matter. When a child or grandchild was in trouble, had to make a career choice, or decide who to marry, the issue was widely discussed among the members of the family. Older members' opinions were sought out, and a decision seemed to be based on some kind of consensus. But now that each generation seems to respect only its own opinions, there is a lessening of communication and support within the total family structure which is damaging to both the older *and* younger generations that comprise it. As a result, young people today often feel isolated and in need of support.

I've also witnessed many embarrassments to members of my own generation as a result of this estrangement, particularly when significant family events totally bypass the elders. To find that major developments in the family—a divorce, a bankruptcy, a public award to a family member—have taken place and the news is brought to the parents by outsiders is quite humiliating to the elders. This is not always due to indifference on the part of the children, however. It may just be that there seemed to be no apparent need to consult the elders, or, perhaps, there was even a desire to spare them pain, unhappiness, or worry. But the end result for the older member is a feeling of exclusion and pain.

While the structure of family authority was being dismantled, social hierarchies—every society's pecking order—were also being "trashed," as the hippies would say. Not only the family and the home, but the schools, the army, and business have always ranked its members in some order. These hierarchies might be based on primogeniture, physical strength, gender, economic status, social status, family connections, religion, skin color, intelligence, or any other variable; but the rankings made sense to those who lived within that particular structure, no matter how irrational or unfair they might seem to outside observers. Everyone accepted his place in the hierarchy. The community functioned well by its rules in the sense that everybody was protected and accounted for.

So far, despite the 1960s, no one has yet formed a society where everybody is equal; the pretense of equality must be enforced through a totalitarian regime such as Russia's communist system. In this country we argue against inequality, but nobody can define equality without the use of some hierarchical concept. We can't all dress the same, look the same, act the same. And nobody really believes absolute equality and sameness is possible or desirable anyway. All social orders are unfair to some of the people, and the hereditary hierarchies are the most unfair, but if any group is to survive and flourish, its individual members must know where they belong. Without an established pattern or style of life, a society will be anger-ridden and chaotic because each trivial act will have to be interpreted as a revelation of the moral philosophy of the individual actor. As T. H. Huxley pointed out, "The doctrine that all men are, in any sense, or have been, at any time, free and equal, is an utterly baseless fiction."

It's hard for members of my generation to digest the extent to which social order has disintegrated during our lifetime. Families are no longer responsible for their own—the government has taken charge of their welfare, as well as that of the less privileged. Earlier in this century, even until the 1930s, the welfare of the impoverished was not so much the government's responsibility as it was the concern of private charities. Furthermore, the abolishment of the pecking order is probably related to a recent lack of effective leaders. Every leader with potential has been chopped down before he could become effective. This has been done through character assassination, at the very least. In any case, without a hierarchical structure, leadership can't easily be established, since every underdog feels cheated because he's not the chosen one, or won't accept the fact that someone else is actually and realistically superior and should rightfully be the leader of the pack. Nothing ever gets done in a non-structured setting, at least not easily, and this country's recent sorry record in government, in industry, and in all aspects of our culture, makes this fact all too plain.

SERMONETTE*

God took the first four Commandments for himself and gave the Fifth Commandment to the parents of the world. But he made no provision for the deification of man. The dictators of the twentieth century, in trying to become gods by abolishing the traditional concepts of God and of fatherhood, killed the Fifth Commandment—all in the name of equality. But they only succeeded in destroying *all* authority, including their own, because the fact is that no mortal man can achieve omnipotence during his lifetime. Only the possibility of a hereafter or a transmigration of the soul can allow for these self-centered expectations.

Is it possible to maintain the family structure intact without adherence to the mandate of the Fifth Commandment to respect our elders? I think not. And since we allowed our leaders to obliterate its message, it is up to us to now try to restore it. But is a restoration of the Fifth Commandment possible outside of a

---

*An attempt will be made to summarize each chapter and to presume to incorporate some moral lesson. I realize this is not the standard practice in a psychiatric book, but I would like to try.

religious context? I would think so, but only if family values are cherished, and only if parents play their roles as intelligent, honorable people.

The family in our society seems lost. We have become less and less committed to our children, parents are less committed to each other, and there is an attitude of permissiveness which encourages indifference and even rebellion. Therefore, as children we ought to be taught to respect those who make sacrifices on our behalf and who contribute to our welfare. More importantly, we must learn to accept responsibility for our own fulfillment and stop blaming parents for our problems.

On the other hand, in some ways it is perhaps just as well that the old pecking order was demolished; it was really quite unfair in many ways. We now have an opportunity to establish a new one, and I hope it will be based on more credible and honorable criteria. Perhaps it will teach us to honor not just our father and our mother, but one another as well.

CHAPTER 2

ON MOTHERING

What Ever Happened
to Molly Goldberg?

*O*ne of the most dramatic events of recent decades was the precipitous downfall of the traditional concept of mothering. Molly Goldberg, the principal character in the popular 1940s and 1950s television show, "The Rise of the Goldbergs," exemplified the now-defunct, old-fashioned mother that, for many of us, embodied many aspects of our own mothers. The show, to which I sometimes contributed ideas, was based on Jewish family value stories with happy endings. The character of the mother, Molly Goldberg, portrayed a warm, nurturing, overprotective mother who took care of everyone in sight and always knew what was best for all. All the wisdom in the world came from her.

But Molly and her brand of mothering lost favor in our new ways of thinking, and her fate is symbolic of the fate of traditional mothering in our society. Her story reflects the effects of social pressures on the old concepts of mothering—pressures that have contributed to dynamic changes in the relationships between the generations. Why did traditional mothering take a fall? What ever happened to Molly Goldberg? This chapter will try to answer those questions.

In the writings of Sigmund Freud, the father is the dominant concern; indeed, he barely mentions his mother at all. But today we are rediscovering our mothers and acknowledging the special problems of identification, separation, and rebellion we experience in relation to them. Contemporary literature reflects a new awareness of mother-daughter relationships (see the works of Vivian Gornick, Nancy Friday, and Mona Simpson, among others). All aspects of mothering have an impact on intergenerational struggles, since changes in the ideals of mothering dramatize very clearly the changes in the world at large.

When I first went into practice over forty-five years ago, soon after getting married, the character of Molly Goldberg still stood for motherhood. The decline and fall of this great maternal figure, as well as the disappearance of similar programs from network television, reveal much of what has happened to the structure of the American family.

On one level, Molly exemplified the Americanization of the immigrant Jews (as well as of other immigrant groups). She was ambitious, upwardly mobile, and literate. More importantly, as a Jewish mother she effectively ruled her family despite the fact that her culture and religion were patriarchal. She was important because it was she who held the family together in adversity.

But by the 1960s, Molly had lost her credibility, becoming the target of derision and even hostility. As the world about her became more prosperous, better educated, less burdened by life, she lost her dominance.

The transition was very rapid. First of all, society decided that Molly didn't know all the answers after all. She herself was the last one to discover that "mother knows best" was no longer an acceptable maxim. All types of authority were being challenged in the 1960s, and hers was no exception. The world was changing very fast and she could not keep up with it. Furthermore, despite her good will, Molly's assumption of omnipotence made other people feel like idiots. Her patronizing smile reflected her sense of superiority over ordinary mortals, as did her habit of offering unsolicited advice. As the men in Molly's life became more and more successful during the postwar period, they began to resent her domination. Her children, too, had moved beyond the limited horizons of the old neighborhood and begun to think they could do without her.

All of these social changes occurred in a world shaped by psychoanalysis. During that period, because Molly had assumed full responsibility for her family, her overprotection was used to explain the failure of introspective, impotent males. She was cited as the cause of all of the guilt and dependency that blocked the inalienable human right to be happy. "Mother" had become a dirty word.

Nonetheless, we all need mothers, and even as Molly's style of mothering declined many other types of mothers rose to replace her. The sexual revolution and the women's movement combined to define new roles for women, many of whom moved out of the home and into the work force. Patterns of mothering presently available as role models are so diversified that I cannot hope to describe them all, but here are a few anecdotal variations of mother types I have come across:

The **Molly Goldberg/Jewish Mother** described above. She's out of fashion now because her family decided it needed to learn to make its own mistakes.

The **Italian/Latin Mother**. Like Molly Goldberg, she's overprotective, with a high level of emotional intensity. But the Italian mother never dominated the men in her family. Instead, she teams up with her daughters to consolidate a solid family. Still in fashion.

The **Screaming Mother**. Not a bad mother, but she tends to over-respond with unrestrained emotion to most situations in daily life, serious and petty, good and bad. In this she is consistent, and the child always knows what she means. She tends to raise good children.

The **German-Jewish/Wasp Mother**. In great contrast to the **Screaming Mother**, the **German-Jewish/Wasp Mother** provides analysts with many of their patients. She specializes in raising children without the expression of emotions. Such a mother is historically related to Victorian and royal mothers whose children were raised by governesses and tutors.

The **Liberal/Intellectual Mother**. She believes in progressive education, the permissive theories of John Dewey, and often misapplies Freudian principles by trying to understand too much and explain away everything. She tries to explain life to her children, instead of teaching them how to live it.

The **Successful Professional/Late-Life Mother**. The late-life mother or career woman. A devoted mother concerned that she joined the party too late and who cherishes the opportunity to parent.

The **Kibbutz/Scandinavian Mother**. She works during her child's infancy, delegating part of its care to members of the community (trained professionals). She believes there is little need for the natural mother when competent help is available. Probably the future of mothering in this country.

The **Poor Working Mother** with the struggling poor husband. The capacity of poor but loving parents to raise well-adjusted children is an amazing example of the power of parental caring and of childhood survival skills.

The **Poor Single Mother**. Her hopeless poverty is a daily tragedy, but sometimes she's able to work a miracle and raise good kids. If she is a teenager whose poverty is compounded by drug addiction, AIDS, or both, her motherhood is a travesty.

The **Prosperous Single Mother**. She represents a new class of liberated women who opt to raise children without fathers. She may have been artificially inseminated. She's too recent a phenomenon to evaluate.

The **Maiden Aunt Mother**. An expression of the maternal instinct which goes back to biblical times: a widowed father marries his dead wife's sister in order to keep the genetic pool intact.

The **Brutalizing Mother** who batters her children. Reports indicate violence breeds only more violence—the children will probably also be physically abusive toward others.

The **Lesbian Mother**. A recent arrival. She seems to function well enough, though not enough time has passed to judge.

The **Male Homosexual Mother**. An emerging group made up of married male homosexuals seeking to become parents, or divorced homosexual fathers seeking custody of their children.

The **Father as Mother**. Apparently, a father can be as good or as bad at mothering as the biological mother.

The **Psychotic Mother**. She is not the same as the **Screaming Mother** because her signals are inconsistent and confused. Rarely does she manage to raise stable kids.

The **Adoptive Mother**. The infertile woman who adopts a needy infant is very common in our society. She and the child almost inevitably face complicated problems.

The **Incestuous or Incest-Permissive Mother**. She's rare, however prominent she may be in the media. There is no more horrendous distortion of parenthood, but the number of children who successfully survive this experience is remarkable. She may prove that any contact, no matter how distorted, is better than no contact at all.

The **Religious Mother**. She has so large a family that she cannot give any single child individual attention. The children raise one another as they did in the nineteenth century, and the parents abdicate personal responsibility, delegating the outcome to the will of God.

The **Alcoholic Mother**. She has always been with us. A horrible mother to her children, a reasonable number of whom nonetheless survive and flourish.

These various models of mothering make two things clear: being a traditional mother is no longer fashionable, and being a child is less of a privilege now than it was in the past.

But Molly's decline didn't only harm the children, for the culture that has less concern for its children also neglects its elders. Molly not only tended her children—she also took care of her widowed uncle. But, in the same way that mothers are no longer expected to care as intensively for their children as Molly once did, today's adult children are no longer expected to care for the elderly members of the family. The problem is that Molly and her husband are apt to live for decades after their children have left home and will most likely need care—but they probably won't get it from their grown children.

SERMONETTE

Although during the 1960s Molly Goldberg's children and grandchildren summarily rejected her authority, many of them are now looking for some of the positive things she once offered.

For instance, women today who would like to commit themselves to motherhood need Molly as a role model; they need to restore the good aspects of traditional mothering that were thrown out along with the bad: the value of selfless giving to a child, for example. In today's materialistic world, new mothers need to understand that helping to form a human life is just as valuable, if not more, than material pursuits like career, money, or success.

Today's men, on the other hand, miss not having a woman like Molly in their lives so they can feel their sexuality is protected. The changes brought on by the sexual revolution and the women's movement, while in many ways positive for women, have made men very unsure of themselves. They often don't know where they stand with today's independent women. Molly, on the other hand, as an unliberated woman, was happily subservient to male authority and hadn't many expectations. She would never dream of questioning the authority of the men in her life or their role in society. In her home, it was clear who wore the pants in the family.

Older men like myself dream of Molly as a nurturing caretaker. After all, what sick or ailing person doesn't want a woman like Molly, who loves to take care of you, wipes your brow, loves and nurtures you? Every sick old man looks for that. Some even marry for that reason alone!

But Molly's brand of mothering is no longer generally acceptable or even available, having been ridiculed and summarily rejected—good and bad—in the past few decades. (Molly herself, however, may not want to take care of her family anymore, anyway. Her children have rejected her and her lifestyle has gone out of fashion. She perceives she's better off without a helpless man who hangs on to her like a child, and she has lost patience with children who cannot resolve their hostility toward her.)

In rejecting Molly Goldberg, we seem to have thrown out the baby with the bath water. If we're not careful, mothering will become a profession in our society, as it already has on the kibbutz and in Scandinavia.

The family misses you, Molly Goldberg!

CHAPTER 3

ON FATHERING

Is Modern Man Obsolete?

*E*ven though modern man was also liberated by the women's movement, his self-esteem has suffered many shattering blows. One thing is for sure: man is no longer the dominant figure that he used to be. His position in our culture has changed; he is no longer expected to "act like a man," and his role as head of the family is almost obsolete. Unfortunately, some men of my generation don't recognize their loss of status, or, if they do, cannot accept it. In those marriages where the father cannot accept this change, bitterness and fragmentation of the family ensues.

In the 1940s, being a man meant having a privileged place everywhere in our society—in the job market, at home, in the family structure, in the political world, in the sexual act. (Although it really wasn't very hard to be superior when women were so passive.) Of course, with these privileges came heavy responsibilities, especially in the roles of father and husband. Substantially, we were living on the edge of the Victorian era—totally unprepared for the rebellions in the offing.

When women began to assert themselves in the 1960s, demanding and achieving greater authority over their lives, men lost much of the control they had previously exercised over their wives, daughters, girlfriends, and mothers. When the younger generation also rebelled in the 1960s, fathers even lost control over their own children, and paternal authority became obsolete.

But men also reaped some benefits as a result of these social developments—their responsibilities were reduced. Men were legally freed from financial responsibility for their adult children and aging parents when the government took over many of what used to be considered the father's responsibilities. Nowadays, it's perfectly legal, and not unusual, for millionaires to have parents and adult children on welfare or receiving food stamps.

In addition, men are now freer to express some traditionally female talents: they are allowed to express their dependency needs, allowed into the kitchen, allowed to cry, allowed to take care of babies. About the only female function man is not expected to assume today is to give birth.

Now that men are freer to be less "manly," it is also easier for them to openly turn to homosexuality, the fear of which has come to replace the old fear of impotence. It took a lot of aggression and responsibility to be a male heterosexual back in the days when women were passive. Now that women are more assertive, it's much easier for a young man to fall into the passive position of homosexuality, which takes no initiative at all. This phenomenon of widespread, out-of-the-closet homosexuality has contributed in recent times to the erosion of the traditional concepts of fatherhood, thus weakening the family structure.

For men who can accept their new status, the release from responsibility has made life much easier: when a man who cannot cope with the burdens of excessive responsibility fails, he is judged less harshly than he once was. Indeed, many men today willingly abdicate their duties toward their children, frequently before those children are even born. Failed marriages and divorce settlements have become much less onerous for the man—alimony is disappearing. These remain devastating events to most women and children, however, who didn't bargain for the abdication of men when they sought their freedom.

So men are no longer the masters. Author Gloria Emerson describes their personal dilemma in *Some American Men*: "At a time when women, with good reason, are asking men to make known their most guarded feelings, when we want them to love us and raise babies and remember our birthdays, it is also required that they be the ones to rescue people in a burning building. And startle the dragons when they are heard in the dark.''

The refusal or inability of many men to accept the changes in their status can also affect them in ways not related to family life. Men live in an entrepreneurial society, and in this arena a man's failures are public knowledge. I believe this is why our present society is so concerned with ostentatious consumption. In our money-oriented world, men express their masculinity by flaunting their possessions, being pretentious, living beyond their means. Status symbols are all that matter, and no one seems to care how they're obtained. Being an honorable man, above suspicion, is a declining value.

These changes in what it means to be a man affect us all. Because the definition of masculinity has become so cloudy, the resulting ambivalence is uncomfortable not just for the men, but for their families and friends as well. After all, we don't stay up to watch old movies because they are so much better than today's, but because we know how we're supposed to feel about the characters—the villains wear black hats, the heroes wear white. The heroines are pretty, wear dresses, act sweet and affectionate, and have breasts; the heroes are aggressive, successful, wear pants, and always pay the check.

Life isn't that simple any more, but we still have to make it work. We need to learn how to live with today's ambiguous gender roles and multidimensional characters because that's the way it is today; the old stereotypes are obsolete. And perhaps it's just as well that competition has left the bedroom to live in the boardroom, where it is separated from biology.

Nonetheless, most children, like their mothers, still look for the image of the respected adult male who acts like a traditional father: he doesn't abandon the family; in the case of divorce, he remains actively involved in his children's life; he provides both emotional and financial support for as long as it's needed.

On the other hand, many men still feel hurt and confused about their less dominant role in the family, and may even feel excluded. When wives and children ask the father for an opinion or advice, he often responds, "I didn't know you cared about my opinion!" For women and young adults to have freedom of choice is a good thing, but we shouldn't throw away the experience and knowledge of generations. Fathers shouldn't be excluded from fathering. Even though male authority has been largely overthrown, men are still the possessors of many unique qualities which are not easily replaced.

SERMONETTE

The traditional masculine role was a joke. Based on the archaic practices of primitive hunting societies, it rapidly lost its meaning once women gained control over their fertility and learned to use the instruments of modern technology. Today, men who try to maintain the male dominant position have difficulties with their wives, children, and grandchildren, and run the risk of becoming remnants of an old civilization. This does not mean that authority is not possible; only that it should not be based solely on gender. If men cannot restore their old dominance, there are many other very human roles left for them to play, based on their intelligence, integrity, leadership abilities, and kindness—none of which are exclusively male.

It is a difficult transition for all of us. Everybody loved the manly image projected by Clark Cable—and many of us want it back! But, sadly, only pieces of him are left, and they are widely distributed among many people of many ages.

None of the complex family problems, none of the sexual problems of women, none of the terrible traumas of being a child in our society can ever come close to resolution unless the self-esteem of the average man can be restored. There is no question that primitive societies still use masculine superiority as the basis of their hierarchical structure—but they have to remain primitive in order to sustain it. Our technological society cannot survive on the morality of the Middle East! However, it also cannot survive without leadership within the family unit. I believe most women and children today would be glad to give up some of their newly-found freedom and strength in exchange for an honest sharing of responsibilities and power.

CHAPTER 4

THE SUCCESSFUL, SELF-MADE FATHER

Good or Evil?

*C*onventional wisdom holds that the successful, self-made father presents a difficult challenge to his children, especially to his sons. It is generally believed that these fathers (and prosperous families in general) can pressure their children so much to succeed and live up to their accomplishments that they doom them to failure. And in some cases this is true, especially among the immigrant families that came to this country in search of a better life and expect their children to continue to struggle for even larger successes than their parents achieved. But by and large, the image of the successful father as an ogre is just not accurate.

Whether true or not, it is usually presumed that the successful father—the villain in this story—became successful by sacrificing the emotional interests of his family. He is supposedly too busy to pay attention to his offspring, too driven and materialistic to be an effective parent, and too demanding of everybody. The children of this stereotypical father presumably become either too discouraged to achieve much themselves or are corrupted by the excessive preoccupation with material possessions they witness in their fathers or families. The wife and mother is torn between loyalty to a husband who, when he's not neglecting her, consumes all of her time, and the emotional demands of her children.

How does this cultural stereotype influence family relationships, especially when his children are not equally successful? Does a successful father always destroy the emotional health of his children? Is it possible that the children would have been better off if their father had been incompetent or a failure? This is constantly implied, as if a parent's achievements could lay a curse on his children. Everybody seems to forget how destructive an incompetent, unemployed, or alcoholic father can be.

There are many reasons why successful fathers have been designated the villains in this reversal of fortunes in family destiny. The most obvious is that it is so much easier to blame successful parents than more pathetic, failing fathers for their children's failures. It is paradoxical, but true, that failure is more acceptable than success in our parents.

Historically, parents have tended to become dependent in their late years on their children. Only in recent years has the equilibrium been disturbed. And most of us have not been too comfortable with the change—older parents because we're no longer taken care of and revered, adult children because their parents are around for much longer and tend to be viewed as a financial and emotional burden. Many people find that it is easier to live with a tragic parent than a successful one because there are less demands and expectations made on the children. This has become even truer since the sexual liberation of the aged and the increased lifespan of our parents; most children can accept the superiority of their fathers, but only because they know their day will come. When the awaited decline of the parent and transfer of power doesn't come—because the father continues to live, to be successful, and to enjoy sex (often with women of his children's age)—the children don't know what to do and develop deep resentments.

We live in a society which fawns over success and celebrity status, making it hard for a father to escape the appearance of presumptuousness if he happens to be very successful. People could hardly wait for Donald Trump to take his fall, and most children cannot wait to challenge the dominance of their powerful, impossible fathers.

But is it possible that our assumptions about successful fathers are just not true? Perhaps it's just a myth that successful fathers destroy the lives of their children. I seriously question whether there truly are more failures among children of prosperous, enterprising fathers than there are in the average family. In fact, there is probably a higher percentage of successful children in high-visibility families, but it seems smaller because there are fewer of these families. And, after all, there are very few truly accomplished people under any economic or social circumstances; failure is just much more obvious, I think, when it occurs in a prominent family. And when it does, everybody is quick to point the accusing finger at the father.

I find it amusing to hear people say that struggle, discipline, or poverty motivate children to success. This is usually pure fantasy. I have known the underprivileged long enough to understand that the painful struggle to survive rarely helps anybody. The lack of privilege and opportunity is a rare incentive for accomplishment. My own experience is that growing up with some privileges will enhance the probability of achieving success, whether it be financial, creative, or emotional.

We still believe the fantasy that good genetics or effective nurturing will guarantee our children the good life. It took a long time to convince us that good heritage was no predictor and that Freud was right when he said that he had no prescriptions for raising an effective child. Life is too complicated; the genetic roll of the dice and the secrets of successful parenting still elude us. So why do we still blame successful fathers when their children are unable to match their achievements? That's too simple a solution.

On the other side of the coin, we find the self-made, prosperous fathers who do develop unrealistic expectations for their children. None of the successful Jewish or Irish men (or members of other underprivileged immigrant groups) I have known seem able to shake the inherent assumptions that form an integral part of the immigrant mentality: the children should achieve a higher status than their parents because they have received an education. This was one of the great dreams that brought the immigrants to this country after centuries of oppression overseas. In the past, this was never a problem—children inevitably achieved more than their parents if properly educated in this country. But these self-made, hardworking men tend forget that once they climb the ladder they might be leaving very little room for their children to climb past them, especially if they are already close to the top. Often, especially in today's economically hard times, their achievements are nearly impossible to match, let alone surpass.

But these successful immigrant families are now living in a purportedly democratic society with level playing fields for all. So why are so many successful, self-made men presuming to establish a permanent, ongoing financial hierarchy? The rage against the impossible successful father is the result. Can't the children slide back without feeling humiliated?

Coming from an immigrant family myself, I commiserated for years with my children, feeling that I was depriving them of the opportunities I had enjoyed: to achieve a higher socioeconomic status than my parents' through education and hard work. Children of privileged parents rarely have the opportunity to experience this heady feeling. My children were born and raised in an already successful, comfortable family, and for them the struggles and challenges I had conquered just didn't exist.

I think that it is an impossible vanity for a self-made man to expect his sons to surpass him. He himself may be just a lucky genetic accident, and there's no guarantee that his children will be as lucky or as talented and able. He would be better off trying to help his children, if they will allow him to. He can always give them—or leave them—money, but in the here and now he should let go of unreasonable expectations and focus instead on the basic moral values that are the ingredients of good family life.

The old-line WASP families, on the other hand, don't seem to have this problem. The continuity of their wealth through the generations and the protection of inherited wealth shields them from the vicissitudes faced by the self-made man. They have the perspective of history; they are aware that the path is not always upward, even with the best of intentions, and know what necessary measures to take to preserve their status.

SERMONETTE

We should all feel compassion for children who fail, whether it be in the financial, emotional, or intellectual arenas. And the resources to encourage a happy result should be available to every newborn in our society. But there are only a very few children born who inherently possess the many talents needed to achieve a big success. No child should be blamed for not possessing these talents.

The proud, hardworking, successful, self-made father is in a position to utilize the fruits of his hard labor to improve life for his family, not to pressure his children to live only to surpass his accomplishments. Actually, it is perhaps fortunate that the successful parent cannot reproduce the same result on command of his progeny; it makes life more challenging and interesting.

On the other hand, most successful fathers don't make impossible demands of their offspring, as is generally believed—quite the contrary. Family life becomes chaotic if the father is always held responsible for his children's successes or failures. Even in the days of royalty, nobody expected every prince to be a great king.

CHAPTER *5*

THE DOWNFALL OF CHILDREN

*T*he golden age of childhood really came to an end in America during the 1960s, when both patriarchy and the family began to unravel almost simultaneously. Nothing devastated my generation more than the discovery that parenthood was not always a blessing. It was quite a shock to discover that, when it comes to raising children, life is often unfair. The Woodstock generation dealt a blow to the good parents along with the bad: children showed mistrust, parents reciprocated, and disenchantment with the state of the world, which had been brewing for some years, suddenly boiled over.

During the European Middle Ages, the child was treated almost like an adult. The family structure served only to transmit life, property, or the family name, and children were apprenticed early on to carry out adult responsibilities. In poorer families, children worked from an early age, often as young as seven, to help support the family. There was little or no education, and few emotional ties existed between children and their parents. This denial of childhood was expressed in the world of art as well. As Philippe Ariès points out in his book *Centuries of Childhood: A Social History of Family Life*, ''Medieval art until about the twelfth century did not know childhood or did not attempt to portray it. It is hard to believe that this neglect was due to incompetency or incapacity; it seems more probable that there was no place for childhood in the medieval world.''

The world continued to treat children without indulgence or even love after the Middle Ages. To a certain extent, this neglect is understandable: any culture engaged in a struggle with survival rarely indulges its children, as witness the children depicted by Dickens in Victorian England, or the persistence of female infanticide in rural China.

Improvements in infant care probably began in the nineteenth century, when the family became a viable unit once fathers began to earn more as a result of the industrial revolution. Mothers and children didn't have to work any more, since father was earning enough for all of them. As Carl Degler says in *At Odds*, ''Exalting the child went hand in hand with exalting the domestic role of woman; each reinforced the other while together they raised domesticity within the family to a new and higher level of respectability.''

The specialization of women into expert, full-time motherhood intensified at the turn of the century, spreading (in theory if not in practice) to the working class. At that time, psychoanalysis, pediatrics, and psychology had begun to consider the needs of children, and our world became obsessed with the physical, moral, and sexual problems of childhood.

Early in my adult life, during the 1930s and 1940s, being a child had become a privilege. That benign attitude toward children reflected widespread prosperity, fewer children, the spread of liberal and progressive educational ideas, and, of course, the influence of Sigmund Freud and Dr. Spock. By the 1950s, being a child was so special that it was treated as if it were an achievement. But these privileges also reflected adult expectations that we could permanently affect the psyche of the child. Only in recent years have we begun to understand how much of the child's temperament is genetic and beyond our control.

Parents of my generation considered themselves guardians of the spiritual and physical health of their children. The family was viewed as more than an institution for the transmission of a name or an estate—it assumed a moral and spiritual function: to mold bodies and souls. Apprenticeship was replaced by education, not only for the oldest sons, but also for younger sons and even daughters. This nurturing, combined with the availability of birth control and a decreasing infant mortality rate, began in the middle class and spread to the poor.

Financially, as well, the role of children had changed. Not only were they no longer expected to make a financial contribution to the family—they became permanent economic burdens to it. Instead of being a source of economic security for aging parents, most children at that time were brought up to feel that they would be provided for eternally. To compound the problem, the adverse economic conditions that followed the 1950s made this generation of children, being brought up to expect so much, significantly less prosperous than its parents.

Largely because of the upheavals of the 1960s and 1970s, our world became disenchanted with parenthood. Adults stopped being so permissive, mothers left the home to go to work, education was neglected and ignored, and youth was disparaged as a wasting asset. But something even worse happened. The younger generation, who had rebelled against its parents during the 1960s, now began to grow suspicious of its own role as parents. The young knew the nature of disenchantment so well that they feared their children would turn against *them* some day. Being good to children (and even having them), which was the hallmark of my generation, went out of fashion. Having children began to seem less important than having a career, and more and more people began to question whether the sacrifices of raising children were worth it.

In many ways to the detriment of today's children, the structure of the family has deeply changed. Fewer middle class and poor parents now raise their own children. More and more children are being raised by single mothers—and 75 percent of them live in poverty. Women's personal and financial needs are now apt to conflict with their maternal functions. Single motherhood doesn't work without economic security, and most women need the structure of marriage to ensure their children's security and well-being. But even that is now subject to no-fault divorce.

Various authors have written on this subject. Vance Packard writes about "our endangered children," and our "anti-child culture"; Neil Postman talks of the "disappearance of childhood"; Marie Winn mentions "children without childhood"; Letty Pogredin asks if Americans hate children; and Germaine Greer tells us that this society is "profoundly hostile to children." More and more commentators talk about children as potentially useful rather than privileged, as having obligations as well as rights.

The days of Dr. Spock, excessive indulgence, and progressive education are over. My generation now realizes that we spoiled our children by not teaching them that getting what they wanted was not a given, but required hard work. So, in some ways, this is good, for children today are being raised differently, held to higher standards. But it also creates a whole new set of problems for them.

Less pampered and indulged, many children today are teetering on the edge of neglect and may now have to face adult problems on their own while they are still quite young. Once they reach the age of twenty-one, parents are no longer really expected to help them in their struggles. (Some studies suggest that by offering a role model for success, a working mother may compensate her children for the lack of personal caring, but this remains to be seen.)

This apparent neglect of children in our times has also had its effects on parents. The present generation of children, being less likely to receive enough emotional support, is, in turn, less capable of giving it. This forces today's elderly parents to rely almost entirely on themselves, their friends, or their community for the support the family used to provide. They can no longer expect to rely on their children in their old age. Well-educated members of my generation have generally not had to rely on their children for economic support; quite the contrary. But emotional sustenance is another story, and in that area nobody gives up hoping. And it's foolishness for disillusioned parents to blame Freud, the communists, the Vietnam war, Dr. Spock, or the Beatles, and just as foolish for hurt and angry children to fault their parents. It's too late to turn the clock back, but we at least can examine and try to understand the changes that have occurred.

As we come into the 1990s, the free-fall of the children seems to be coming to an end. An awareness of our failures as parents seems to be mounting. Unlimited permissiveness is no longer acceptable. We are expecting more from our children and hopefully they will respond. But are we willing to offer them the ingredients—communication, concern, nurturing—which will make it possible for them to mature in a responsible fashion?

SERMONETTE

The bitterness of parents following the rebellion of the 1960s is waning. Molly Goldberg will probably never return, but mothering is being rediscovered everywhere. Today's mothers are very impressive in their dedication, in their utilization of every possible resource. Many are insisting on being mothers, and good ones, whether a man is available or not. On the other side of the coin, the collapse of the financial markets has deeply affected men. The chase of the dollar is being reevaluated, and many men seem to be returning to human values. Being a good father seems to be one of them.

Perhaps the family can begin to return to values which are acceptable to three or four generations simultaneously. Then, perhaps, we can all talk to each other in the same language at last, and our children will feel loved and supported again.

CHAPTER *6*

THE PURSUIT OF HAPPINESS

I would like to propose that the concept of ''the pursuit of happiness,'' as applied to child-rearing, has been one of the causes of many serious family problems. When I was young, life was considered cruel, and survival—not happiness—was the first priority, particularly during the Great Depression. We felt lucky to survive the rise of Hitler and the Second World War.

But all of this changed for our children due to the prosperity of the 1950s and the emergence within the family of the concept of the pursuit of happiness. As a result of the good fortune we were enjoying, we didn't think to explain to our children the importance of what we'd been through and the lessons we'd learned from it all: that happiness, like freedom, is something that has to be earned, and sometimes even fought for; it will not be automatically bestowed upon anyone.

Until the American and French revolutions of the late-eighteenth century, no government had ever promised the people happiness. The average person was lucky if the government allowed them to breathe. Not until the Declaration of Independence was the pursuit of happiness listed as an inalienable right.

What Jefferson and the other signers of the Declaration of Independence had in mind, however, was that a government should guarantee its people liberty, safety, and access to opportunity—not enjoyment, self-esteem, contentment, or unlimited rapture. As Freud wrote in *The Death Instinct*, "the intention that man should be 'happy' is not in the 'Creation'." And Joseph Campbell, in *The Hero with a Thousand Faces*, says about Greek tragedy: "The happy ending is justly scorned as misrepresentation; for the world, as we know it, as we have seen it, yields but one ending: disillusionment, and ironic unfulfillment galls the blood of even the envied of the world!"

Nevertheless, after World War II, having successfully survived the horrors of the Hitler era and experiencing an unprecedented prosperity, we began to believe that we could promise our children almost anything, including happiness. My generation's optimistic dreams all seemed to be coming true: science and rationality seemed ascendant, Einstein was a hero, prosperity seemed to be permanently here, we were enthralled with our understanding of psychoanalysis. We thought we had all the answers. Children became priceless; every parent I knew was ready to enroll his children in the Garden of Eden, offering them unlimited pleasures with seemingly no expectation in return. We advised our children: "Do what will make you happy!" Sexual freedom was possible and sin went out of style.

But during the 1960s, the "fall and banishment" was painful for everybody. From our children's point of view, life seemed somehow wrong: there were no challenges, no more frontiers. If they fled west, they ended up in Haight-Ashbury. Their parents spoke like liberals, but their values were materialistic. The country lost its direction: we couldn't deal with the demands of blacks, we got involved in wars we could not win, political leaders seemed ineffectual, popular leaders were assassinated.

As the children of the postwar period grew into adult life, our dreams started to disintegrate. We'd guaranteed them effortless happiness, but they'd found that real life outside the family didn't work that way. Few had been educated to hard work; they'd spent their childhoods expecting to be eternally happy. Without work skills, they could not find fulfillment in the real world. They were either confused about what to do or forced to go into the family business. Either way, they were always angry with their parents. Their sexual freedom gave them only the chance to have sex without commitment, which separated sex from love. Without the capacity to work on a dedicated level it's hard to find lasting happiness. Our disappointed children turned to the Beatles and to pot.

The 1960s generation tried to find its happiness in drugs and loveless sex, without commitment to work. When happiness didn't materialize, they turned on their parents and blamed them. And they were right. Nobody should promise to make another person happy. Your happiness is something you have to earn yourself. Even the offer of eternal parental love has no meaning to a child if the child doesn't reciprocate it.

Happiness is an unpredictable happenstance, an occasional by-product; it should never be a direct goal. When a friend asked me why my sons had turned out to be so successful, I answered that my advice to them had been: "Just work hard and go into areas that you think you can accomplish something in. You're going to be miserable at times. But don't try to be happy. When you're good at something, that's when you'll be truly happy. When you have a good job or a good marriage you're happy—but you have to work very hard at it."

We had nurtured the Woodstock generation on empty promises of permissive happiness. Now the tables are turned. The myth of effortless happiness we taught our children is now deluding *us* with false promises: that we can have unlimited social support, eternal sex, vigor forever, devoted children always. Consequently, older people who don't have all of these things seem as disappointed as the adolescents of the 1960s. Growing older is not, in itself, any great tragedy. Everything that can go wrong in later years can also go wrong earlier on in our lives. We cannot afford to delude ourselves into believing that the problems of life can be solved by denial and impossible dreams. This is what we should have learned from our children's rebellion.

SERMONETTE

We all know that happiness is more than merely the avoidance of pain. It encompasses an awareness of self, a recognition of the natural world, the use of intelligence, and a sense of mastery, effectiveness, and competence in work as well as in our personal relationships. During the 1960s, our children placed much emphasis on feelings, on "letting it all hang out." Unbridled passion and sloppy mindlessness, aided and abetted by drugs, ruled the day. But an effective life is based on planning and foresight; nothing works by itself. Every relationship, emotional or economic, has to be periodically renewed. Spontaneity does not work as a solution: if we don't plan intelligently, if we can't manage to repair a bridge until it collapses, we are indeed in trouble. Human passions are always contaminated by greed, envy, and hostility; they alone cannot be used to shape our destinies. We need to use intelligence as the basis for planning our futures. And we need to teach our children this.

The passive expectation of happiness is one of the tragedies of the past forty years. Without stretching the truth too much, it is possible to conceptualize the whole illegal drug problem as a manifestation of the search for pleasure without performance, elation without involvement. Happiness has been converted into an entitlement.

The older generation today sets its children a bad example when it withdraws from a functional life in old age and calls it happiness—a lifetime of being effective is thrown away to do nothing. Both Freud and Voltaire considered hard work to be the only antidote to old age.

Whether it be in old age or in adolescence, "the inalienable right to the pursuit of happiness" will only be fulfilled if the pursuit itself is based on effectiveness and the nurturing of a meaningful life, preferably within a family.

CHAPTER 7

SHOULD CHILDREN LOVE THEIR PARENTS?

"Children begin by loving their parents. After a time they judge them. Rarely, if ever, do they forgive them."

Oscar Wilde, *A Woman of No Importance*

A bout forty years ago, one of the guests at a dinner party at my home asked, "Does anyone in this room really enjoy being with his parents?" Seven psychiatrists and their spouses were there, and the question shocked us all. So did the fact that only one person in the room was honestly able to answer, "Yes, I do." The rest of us insisted that we did our duty by our families, but we couldn't describe it as anything more than that. Some of us even said that being with our parents was painful.

Since we were all raising our own families at the time, we went on to speculate whether our children would one day feel the same way about us. One of the more distinguished members of the group predicted quite definitely that our children would find us far more acceptable than we did our own parents. After all, we were better educated, more prosperous, and more American than our immigrant parents.

How wrong he was! If anything, we get along less well with our adult children than our parents did with us. The present generation of older people enjoy less and less meaningful contact with the middle generation, and this estrangement has affected all of our relationships. Everyone I talk to about it reports a breach between the generations, a fragmentation of the family unit.

Of course, intergenerational strife is not new—look at Oedipus, or King Lear. What is different today is that added to the generation gap are a fragmentation of the family as a whole and the dissolution of old values. My generation is healthier, longer-lived, and more prosperous than its predecessors, but our sense of loneliness is pervasive, especially among mothers.

Having been exposed to many older ladies in recent years, I am struck by the complex ways in which widows try to disguise their problems with their adult children. Almost nobody in my generation, men or women, seems prepared to face up to the complexity of intergenerational problems, but women seem to avoid the subject even more.

A woman friend of mine was very proud of her physician son's achievements and her role in his development. She was in constant contact with him, and they did their financial planning together, utilizing the mother's financial and legal skills. In fact, at times I was envious of what she had achieved in relation to her son—until it finally dawned on me that she never really saw him. Their conversations were all night-time phone calls, collect from him to her. She was in fact very isolated, while nevertheless providing for his financial future. I much preferred my own abrasive but frequent and direct confrontations with my family.

Why are relationships between elderly parents and their middle-aged children so difficult today? The same problems have certainly existed in other times and cultures, and we've read about the horrendous solutions that primitive tribes found for taking care of their infirm or elderly, especially in the early hunting societies. But we don't do much better ourselves. Today we are perhaps more civilized in the ways we detach ourselves from our aged, but most frequently we do this by simply putting them away in a hospital or nursing home, where they are barely kept alive, with a plastic tube in every orifice, unable to speak because of a laryngeal tube, and usually in coma, anyhow. We rarely visit, let alone keep them at home with us.

The truth is, in this country, anyway, that people have become less committed to one another. This is obviously a glib oversimplification, but I honestly believe it. People today seem to be less attached to one another than in times past; we care less about what happens to the other person. We just seem to give less of a damn.

These developments are more important, more profound, although also more subtle, than many of the dramatic upheavals of the past few decades. The changes in sexual roles and the increase in the divorce rate are both secondary to the loss of commitment. And there is no doubt that one of the causes of our indifference toward one another is diminished loyalty within the family as a whole.

The bonds of caring are breaking in all areas of our society: lovers are less faithful to each other, business partners trust each other less, friends rely less on one another. Marriages are less stable, resulting in families being more fragmented: children feel less responsible for their aging parents; parents in general feel less responsible for their children. An adult child is no longer legally responsible for the care of his parents, nor are the parents responsible for any incompetent child. Thirty years ago, 50 percent of adult children helped their parents financially, as required by law. Now that figure is down to 4 percent; most states no longer hold parents responsible for the welfare of their children.

This lack of caring has multiple causes: first, people are living longer (enough said—longer life multiplies all problems); second, we brought up this generation permissively and expected less of them and, logically, we are getting less back; third, the revolts of the 1960s disrupted family loyalties because the traditional family was summarily rejected along with all other forms of authority; fourth, my generation tends to be more prosperous than our children's (we had the advantages and opportunities of the postwar boom, while our children live in less fortunate times), and a well-to-do parent does not evoke tenderness or caring like a poor, pathetic, immigrant mother or father; and fifth, over the past thirty years financial responsibility for the aged has increasingly been assumed by the public sector (Social Security, pension funds, and governmental agencies now exist that were unheard of when my generation was young), thus, children no longer feel that supporting their aged parents is their responsibility—the government is supposed to do it for them.

In the 1940s, most children came into therapy because they were suffering acute distress from anxiety, phobia, and fear of abandonment. Their anxious parents were concerned for their children and felt guilty about failing them. Nowadays, the picture has changed. The children tend to be indifferent and the parents are the frightened ones. In one generation, fear has shifted from child to parent.

As for adult neuroses, these too have changed. We used to take care of anxious patients who were phobic or obsessive, who were torturing themselves, not others. Now, borderline and psychopathic personalities fill our offices. The hysteria of the nineteenth century has been replaced by the schizo-affective state. Detachment, rather than dependency, is the hallmark of today's neuroses; the old neurotic behavior reflected fears of separation or of unfulfilled needs because in those days we were all more dependent on one another. In my parents' home as well as in my own, for example, children were never left casually, with baby sitters. But modern guiltless psychopaths don't fear loss—they've never had much to lose. As family ties began to loosen, as family members felt less committed to one another, dependency began to be perceived as undesirable. Self-sufficiency became the new ideal, which, on a personal level, translates into narcissism. Glorifying the self, putting your own wishes above anyone else's, means you deny the fact that anyone has ever done anything worthwhile for you.

But no one can truly blossom in isolation. In primitive societies, the ultimate punishment for serious transgressions was ostracism. Today, we are apparently choosing to ostracize ourselves: in 1985, 20.6 million Americans were living alone—twice as many as in 1970.

Nobody can be born, survive, grow, or prosper outside some kind of a family, that practical institution designed to ensure human survival. In its early days, the family provided a way for couples to live apart and thus avoid the mayhem caused by conflicts within the family. Once conditions improved so that infant survival was possible, women didn't die as often in childbirth, and there was enough to eat, family members had the luxury of loving one another, and a pattern of family life evolved in our culture that was regarded, when I started to practice, as normal, reasonable, and civilized: Two partners of opposite sexes lived together for an indefinite period and had several children who lived at home until they grew up. Various animals were usually part of the household, and grandparents, uncles, aunts, and cousins lived close by.

But this nuclear family structure has eroded in the last thirty or so years. There has been a significant trend toward isolation: when the "yuppies" appeared in the 1980s, it became every man for himself, and each in his own world. The number of single-parent households keeps increasing. Margaret Mahler and Selma Fraiberg in this country, and John Bowlby, Anna Freud, and D. W. Winnicott in England have documented the unhappy results of this individuation-separation. And Harry Harlow has demonstrated the demoralizing effect of isolation on the future emotional behavior of macaque monkeys, making it clear that the adult capacity to love can be destroyed by disappointment in infancy.

And yet, while nobody wants to be alone, we continue to separate ourselves from one another. People complain about feeling cut off from family, about loneliness, more than they complain about bad health. They yearn for a connection. "Only connect," as E. M. Forster said. An ad in a New York City community newspaper read: "Family alienation: A support group for parents who have become alienated from their adult children has been formed . . . All are welcome."

In spite of all this, I ask the question, Should children love their parents? The Fifth Commandment requires us only to honor and respect—maybe love is too much to demand. After all, why should we expect children to love parents who have forced them into becoming civilized? What child can love the mother who weans him from the breast? or who toilet trains him? or who makes him learn the multiplication tables? or who makes other, truly impossible demands on him? As a patient of mine once complained to me, "Doctor, I don't understand. You expect me to feel love for my mother when I find her to be impossible; in fact, I find it hard to explain just how much she offends me."

Probably the most difficult family problem seen in practice these days is just that—parents making impossible demands on adult children who have no way of satisfying the needs of their parents. Older parents remember the old days, when families lived in larger groupings and it was always possible to find an extra pair of hands to sustain a failing parent. But the demographics have changed; families are widely scattered into smaller units and children have not been nurtured on any substantial sense of responsibility. And even with all the good will in the world, many well-intentioned adult children have neither the resources nor the capacity to meet their parents' expectations. In office practice, it is a most difficult problem, and it is imperative to determine how much each child can give and still live with his or her conscience at the funeral.

And yet we all lose from not behaving responsibly and with respect toward one another—parents and children. As adult children, we should understand that even though our parents were far from perfect we should treat them with respect and care for them to the best of our ability, like they did for us when we were growing up. As elderly parents, we should consider that perhaps we expect too much—when love is not forthcoming, perhaps caring and respect will do.

I was very impressed recently when I saw a television documentary about Japanese family life in which one family was portrayed at home. The daughter-in-law expressed her hatred of the husband's mother, but accepted as a fact of life that the mother-in-law was the authority in the household. And that household did work. People don't have to love one another, just act civilized and show respect.

SERMONETTE

Many children are relieved when they realize that it may not be necessary to love and nurture their parents. They come to learn that this has nothing to do with respect or caring for their parents' needs in their later years. Loving and caring are two different emotions. The Fifth Commandment says nothing about loving—only honoring. Every adult child has a "story" to justify his anger with his parents. But despite this, it is important that they learn to be attentive, because if they fail to do so, they may be imprinting a pattern which they may regret at a future date, since their own children will tend to follow the example they have witnessed.

CHAPTER *8*

THE REVERSAL OF THE FIFTH COMMANDMENT

*T*he changes in the hierarchy within the family and the dismantling of family closeness has been devastating for many members of my generation. Many parents are unaware of how universal the problem is. Some live in terror of losing contact with their grandchildren; others feel ashamed because they know their contemporaries think they have failed as parents. Some believe the family estrangement is a symptom of their personal failure.

This sense of alienation between elderly parents and adult children is escalating. One of my sons (in his forties), upon his return from a high school reunion, commented that many of his friends, who had been a part of the 1960s hippie movement, had managed to carve out successful careers—but few of them had managed to reconcile with their families.

It seems very curious to me how children can feel so free to abdicate their status as members of the family. After all, the Fifth Commandment says that children should honor their father and mother. But it seems to have been reversed—it's now the father and mother who seem driven to obligate to honor their children, in the hope of restoring traditional values.

It is my impression that the way most children feel about their parents depends on the image that the parents project. My children always seemed to feel closer to my wife and me when they were able to feel proud of us in front of their friends. All children would like to be proud of their parents, but so few are able to. When they are, the effect can be dramatic.

One patient of mine was seventy-eight years old and thought he had a good relationship with his children, who visited with him occasionally and always treated him with due deference and concern for his health. But the children had active lives of their own, and he was rarely included in their social activities. Tempted to complain, he refrained, remembering only too well that his own relationship with his widowed mother had been no different.

A dramatic change occurred one Thanksgiving, when some of his daughter's friends were included in the family festivities and he took part in a discussion about music with them. He became quite animated—music had always been his passion, and his knowledge of it was encyclopedic. On the following day, the family called quite excitedly to let him know that he had been the hit of the party. They had always taken his interests and knowledge for granted, but when they saw him through their friends' eyes, they became impressed with him again. His status rose and his family began to use him to improve theirs.

But things aren't always so easy to turn around. When the family won't change, I offer another solution to my patients. One of them, a woman in her sixties, never saw her daughter despite the fact that she and her two children lived in the same metropolitan area. My patient's phone calls went unanswered, and all holidays, including Mother's Day, were disregarded. The daughter gave no excuses and no explanation for this, and we were unable to accomplish a reconciliation over a period of time. We then discussed the possibility of finding a new family for her. Rejected by her own, I encouraged my patient to adopt a new one. There are plenty of children who may have been rejected by their original families and are eager to find a surrogate parent. My patient had a lot to offer, and did manage to find people who were willing to accept her.

Yet another alternative I would like to suggest is that we undo the reversal of the Fifth Commandment. What would happen if parents stopped honoring their rejecting adult children and abdicated from their roles as parents? What would the parents lose, since they already feel deserted anyway? This actually works quite well in practice. I have suggested this ploy to some of my patients and the results are quite dramatic, since most children are quite unprepared to accept rejection by their parents; some suddenly become aware of how unfair they have been. This technique can help to shake the children up, precipitate a proper amount of guilt, and lead to substantial changes.

There are many situations where the parents can refuse to allow themselves to be exploited. For example, if their adult children have drug abuse problems, parents can decide not to allow themselves to be bankrupted emotionally and financially; they can instead give up responsibility and turn to public assistance for solutions.

Perhaps the most difficult situations are those in which the grandchildren are being held hostage by their parents until the grandparents provide financial assistance: the elderly parents are threatened with total isolation if they do not accede to their children's demands. I have been witness to some victims successfully threatening to give up their privileged positions as parents—abdicating—unless given their due. Under these conditions, everybody becomes shaken, and relationships may then improve.

To use this strategy effectively, I've suggested to some of my patients that a simple statement, without anger, is enough—no need for dramatics. Suddenly, the parents are able to leave the bondage of their shame. If they have no money, they can turn to their peers or the public sector for assistance and face up to the fact that they cannot depend on their own family. If they do have money, a viable marriage, and friends, they free themselves to live without unreasonable responsibilities to the younger generation. And, if they're lucky, they can eventually achieve with their children a relationship based on mutual respect.

Actually, many of my friends find their adult children boring. Why should they struggle to keep up relationships with them, especially when the children act superior? Most of the matters that preoccupy the young are situations their parents have already lived through, solved, and left behind years ago. Even so, their children refuse to concede their parents can help in any way.

SERMONETTE

I feel it's morbidly obsolete and totally unacceptable—in therapy as well as in real life—to blame and harass parents for a child's every deficiency, especially once the child's grown up. We know too much about child development now. We've learned that a great deal of others' behavior is beyond anyone's control because it's tied to constitution, temperament, and genetics. However, parents are still being held responsible for their children's failures, and many parents crumble under the assault.

The absence of much needed love and attention from their offspring can be devastating for most parents. There has to be a better way to resolve these problems if we are to preserve the family. This is possible only if we accept the premises of the original Fifth Commandment. If this is not possible, there is no point in trying to be a parent.

CHAPTER *9*

A THANKSGIVING DAY SERMON

We gather each year to celebrate Thanksgiving, a national holiday to commemorate the arrival of the Pilgrims, and to express gratitude for the plentifulness of their newly-adopted country. It is a very special day for parents, for, more than anything else, we are celebrating the importance of our own families

Thanksgiving is *the* American family holiday. Everybody returns home for this occasion, and it is unique as the only day in the year when we all seem capable of getting together without protest. It's the one day when all the progeny congregate in one room and the older generation is almost certain to see their offspring. It's a tribute to our tradition that this holiday encompasses so many of the older immigrant participants, who perhaps would feel closer to an Israeli, Irish, or Scandinavian celebration. But we're all here, no matter what our origins and our differing religions. It's really a wonderful holiday.

Other holidays seem to have less meaning for families—at least to my own. During Christmas, it seems harder to get together; too many of us are on our way south to the Caribbean or north for skiing. For July Fourth we may be at the Hamptons; Easter Sunday and Passover Seder are sometime events. The religious revival seems to have skipped this family, but Thanksgiving remains.

44

Around Thanksgiving time, the school children are on vacation and seem anxious to return home; it is time for the college students to touch base again. It's hard to get them back to school after this brief visit. They seemed so eager to get away to school that it's nice to have them back seemingly more appreciative of their home base. The middle generation looks forward to being with their children and their seniors simultaneously.

But why does something always go wrong at Thanksgiving celebrations? In fact, the Friday after Thanksgiving is usually one of the saddest days of the year, if I judge by my psychiatric practice. Whatever is happening, this ultimate family holiday usually runs into trouble. Something just doesn't seem to work.

Possibly our attempts to recapture the kind of holiday evoked by Norman Rockwell's illustrations of Thanksgiving Day dinner in the *Saturday Evening Post* are unrealistic. Our expectations seem to exceed our performance. It's an ongoing embarrassment; we seem to be trying to recreate something that may not have ever existed for us—maybe it never did for anybody. But it looked and sounded so good . . .

Certainly within our lifetime most families seem to have become less cohesive. Everybody is looking for the family, but it seems not to be out there anymore. Each marriage is a family unit on its own. The extended family seems to be losing its connections, and now we have to face the phenomenon of some of our single women having children on their own, without marriage or visible husbands.

The big problem is that we have such a terrible record when it comes to keeping the family together; we are trying to continue to celebrate an institution which was almost abolished during the 1960s. The mother still hasn't recovered from the emotional thrashing she received during the hippie revolution; she hasn't gotten over the fear that her children will yell at her or disappear overnight.

We all have tried very hard to preserve our families, but the times were against us. It's nobody's fault, but we cannot take our family problems for granted anymore. I remember our last Thanksgiving. It was a disaster. We were lucky that we didn't end up in a fistfight. Sam, my father-in-law, who unfortunately passed away last year, couldn't resist making defensive Jewish remarks which seemed directed against Mary, our lovely Italian daughter-in-law. She took it quite well—but why was she acting like a sibling toward our granddaughter? All I ask this year is that everybody control themselves during the meal; we will invite you back later in the season to settle family differences individually.

Nothing is more threatening to the average American family than to bring all of its members together in a sort of pressure cooker—Thanksgiving dinner—and to force them to enjoy one another's company and act as if they are one big, happy family. It used to be easier when the older generation commanded some respect, but those days are long gone. Siblings may have civilized feelings toward one another, but feel no obligation to act as if they do. Everybody seems to be living out their unresolved sibling rivalries these days. Daughters-in-law and sons-in-law feel no obligation to behave with courtesy when they are not restrained by members of the family. Grandchildren can be cute, but they often take their cues from the worst-behaved members of the family.

We used to have great families; what happened to them?

I would not be talking this way unless I believed we would all like to have happy families again. None of us quite knows how to accomplish this, but I think the onus is going to be on us to do some hard work. Let's face it; we all broke up the family and we will all have to work to repair it. Since the 1960s, we haven't been trained to act as a family. We have raised our children since then as if the family unit were composed of one—the child.

Our children are afraid to make demands of their children; they remember their own rebellion and are afraid that it will repeat itself. But if we don't return to some aspects of tradition, with all the risks involved, the alternative is chaos.

The solution for Thanksgiving is quite simple. It should be played as theater piece. Each member of the family should be provided with a script outlining the expected behavior and dialogue of each of the attendants assembled. It is quite easy to act like a civilized family if everybody recognizes that the charade will be brief, that it's only make-believe, and that it won't be repeated for another year. It can then become a constructive exercise in self-control.

Nobody should really attend this occasion unless they are prepared to play their role. After all, being a family used to be a kind of charade. If repeated often enough, it can even become quite real. People do enjoy playing games together, but if they don't play by the rules, the scenario can disintegrate. Problems arise only when they believe that the games are a substitute for life. Feel free to be yourselves the rest of the year. Once a year is enough for a beginning.

SERMONETTE

It's really not that hard to be a family once a year when we're together on Thanksgiving. It's worth the try, and is a small repayment to one's parents, who try so hard to maintain the myth of family tradition. It's also a good example for the little ones, and it may even take with the oncoming generations, unless new Woodstock rebellions intervene.

CHAPTER 10

POLONIUS WAS WRONG
The Concept of Quid Pro Quo

Neither a borrower nor a lender be;
For loan oft loses both itself and friend,
And borrowing dulls the edge of husbandry.
This above all—to thine own self be true,
And it must follow, as the night the day,
Thou canst not then be false to any man.

Shakespeare, *Hamlet* I, iii

*P*olonius' words seem to have infiltrated our family relationships even to this day. He has given borrowing and lending a bad reputation for too long a time. Frequently quoted as an example of Shakespeare's wisdom, these words have provided many people with a justification for their indifference towards other family members. Although both parents and children constantly protest their virtue in their dealings with one another, the facts often belie their need to appear honorable. Since most of us will need our families throughout our lives, we should try to find a way to relate to one another with honesty and open reciprocity.

Even if Polonius were talking only about money, he's given many people a convenient excuse for being stingy in a variety of other ways; I'm afraid that his cautions have also spread to the currency of emotions. More and more people seem to deal with one another as if they were afraid of the warnings in Polonius' words. In our world of increasing loneliness and isolation, family members have no choice but to be freer in exchanging whatever we have to offer, and to take whatever is available. The problem lies in the *nature* of the exchange: Is it reciprocal? Does it adhere to the *quid pro quo* principle?

The problem with exchanges between people (whether monetary or otherwise) is that they tend to be one-directional; some people are always taking, others always giving.

We all have a prejudice in favor of the benefactor rather than the recipient: "It is more blessed to give than to receive." (Acts 20:35) But my experience is quite to the contrary—I think it is perhaps more difficult to find a gracious receiver than a generous donor. My years of practice as a psychoanalyst have shown me that there are more people who are generous givers than there are talented recipients.

No relationship can survive for very long without adhering to the *quid pro quo* principle. Thus, the real problem is how to find a person, or a couple, capable of being both—giver and gracious receiver—either simultaneously or in sequence. People have to give something back, however intangible, even if it's only the capacity to receive graciously. Nobody can be neither a giver nor a taker without eventually becoming estranged from the world in which he lives. Money, love, strength, pleasure, concern, solitude, caring, respect, intelligence, submission—these are some of the currencies of human interchange. We all have to exchange these with one another in some form in order to live, to work, to be part of a family, to grow old.

We are all vain beyond human comprehension; we are beggars from the beginning. The question is not how noble we are, but if we play the game fairly. Have we earned our rights or are we demanding a free ride?

This has always been a special problem for me. The recipient of great concern and generosity during my younger years, I have also been in a position to play the giving role in adult life and have tried to balance the books. But I quickly discovered that there was no way I could help to support everybody within my personal horizon. An obvious mark, it was necessary for me to develop a keen sense of reciprocity in order to survive. After many years, I discovered that I became emotionally drained when I didn't receive something in return—it's easy to bankrupt the account if all transactions are withdrawals and nothing is deposited. (My wife was no problem; she knew how to take graciously and brought me many treasures in return.)

Reasonable people are aware that the return doesn't have to be in kind: an adolescent can reward you for your generosity by doing his homework or keeping his room clean; a patient can reciprocate by getting better or paying his bill; a friend can be supportive during bereavement.

The *quid pro quo* principle applies to children as well. Should a child be forever entitled to unconditional love? Can a parent give continual love without some return—in the form of tenderness or performance—without some reciprocity? How much rebelliousness is acceptable during adolescence? When should a parent's complete dedication to his children cease once the children reach adulthood? Should life always be a one-way street for parents?

For many adult children the reverse is true: When should they stop feeling responsible for their failing parents? What are the limits of responsibility to the older generation, especially when they grow cranky and sometimes even abusive? (I can, however, testify to the fact that it is very hard to avoid becoming a cranky old man; it is a tough struggle, more so when the only reason for being irritable is the sheer fact of growing older. Becoming angry is the last bastion of ineffectual self-assertiveness against the advancing of the years.)

SERMONETTE

According to biblical wisdom, a good person should be capable of generosity to others without expecting any meaningful return instantly, or in the foreseeable future. It is considered in very poor style to be so selfish as to be generous only in the expectation of future rewards. If this is true, I guess I don't know any really decent people, because everybody I know, including myself, seems to expect some returns in this life. There's a lot of bitterness about these days, especially among members of the older generation, who feel that very little of their generosity has been reciprocated. All of us tend to feel guilty about having such feelings, but I'm quite convinced that they are irresistible. I don't think that I'm all that different from the rest. The world is just not that perfect.

In the struggle between the generations, the problem of who takes and who gives is endless. There is little question that under ordinary circumstances the giving and the nurturing travel from grandparents, to adult children, to grandchildren in a downward spiral, and this is as it should be. We presume that reciprocity is accomplished by the flowing back of caring, loving, devotion, and respect, but something always seems to be going wrong. Unless we set clear rules of exchange based on the concept *quid pro quo* early on in the family, we will end up drowning in a sea of dissatisfaction and resentment.

In his great tragedy, Shakespeare put the offending words used to open this chapter into the mouth of the pompous Polonius. Would that he could have advised instead:

> One should a borrower, or a lender be;
> For loan oft gains both itself and friend,
> And borrowing sharpens the edge of husbandry.
> This above all—to thine own self be true,
> And it must follow, as the night the day,
> Thou canst not then be alone with any man.

CHAPTER *11*

THE ECONOMIC FACTOR

*T*here are many economic reasons why the problems between adult children and their parents have become more complex: a longer lifespan creates the need for money to support aging family members; conflicts between the more prosperous older generation and its children, who were brought up with unreasonably high expectations; differing attitudes about money between the generations (even as the younger generation's income is decreasing, they are spending more and saving less than their better-off parents ever did); and government subsidies for the aged, funded largely through taxes on the young and middle aged.

Historically, the economic norm in this country has been that of upward mobility. In previous centuries, children usually became more prosperous than their parents, and were able—and willing—to become financially responsible for them. Families back then took care of their own. But while these old patterns still persist somewhat, things are changing.

In the past few years, I've heard middle-aged children express envy toward their parents because they had been able to buy homes, live "the American Dream," and even accumulate an estate. In the 1950s, a husband's moderate income would support a wife, three or four children, an automobile, a four-bedroom house with an attic, basement, and picture window, a TV set, a back yard barbecue grill, sirloins every Saturday night, and a three-week summer vacation at the seashore every summer. Families lucky enough to have two incomes could also buy a summer house at Cape Cod or take the whole family to Europe.

But today, because tax laws have changed, Wall Street took a tumble, and money is not so easily kept, children cannot live the way they did when they were growing up. To live in their parents' lifestyle, the working partner in a one-income family today would have to be a partner in a Wall Street firm or otherwise be able to count on a six-figure salary. Otherwise, both partners would have to be working full-time.

Let's also take a look at the matter of Social Security. Many Americans are convinced that later generations will never collect on the Social Security taxes they must now pay. The aged, now a powerful pressure group in our society, successfully fight any cuts in Social Security at the expense of other programs. In 1987, President Reagan stated that no spending was exempt from budget cuts—except old age assistance. There were a few passing comments to the effect that frequent cuts in education are destroying the hopes of future generations. But cutting funds for education and other programs is still considered an acceptable mode of reducing spending—as long as Social Security is left untouched. The beginnings of a backlash are becoming apparent.

Patterns of spending are also different now, but here it is the aged who tend to envy their children's freedom with money. Socially, the price of admission today is high. In my generation, people met mostly in their homes; that's how I met my wife. Nowadays, you're always expected to go to some expensive formal dinner or event. In some families, the parents stay home, unable or unwilling to pay the price of the current social scene, envying their children, who have no hesitation about spending what to the parents are excessive amounts of money on entertainment and social events.

These changing economic conditions undoubtedly contribute to intergenerational tensions. The generation that was raised during those years of prosperity, when only the father worked and everyone owned a home, is now middle-aged and resentful of the fact that their standard of living is lower. Because they were born during a time of heady victory, success, and economic growth, they grew up thinking they would always be taken care of, have anything they desired, and live as well or better than their parents and grandparents. Unfortunately, these middle-aged children never learned to adjust to their reality, and many have no compunction about how they get the money they think they're entitled to: they may get involved in shady stock trading or in other illegal enterprises, or, as the *New York Times* recently reported, they may exploit the older people in their families. They may even blackmail their parents by threatening to keep them from seeing their grandchildren unless they agree to subsidize the grandchildren's education or otherwise contribute money.

SERMONETTE

The family is a wonderful institution: it protects us from isolation, ensures continuity, and looks after the economic welfare of its members. But the expectation of money without the individual effort of each member can be a very disenchanting experience. For the good of all involved, parents of ordinary means have to train their children to become self-sufficient once they leave the family.

Middle-aged children caught up in the bind of resentment and attempted exploitation of their previous privileged positions must realize that what their parents achieved and shared with them was usually earned through great effort. It's hard to tell them that they may have to do the same. However, they may have the uneasy comfort of knowing that they share this problem with a whole generation—they are not alone.

Envy of wealthy parents is not a new phenomenon; it's always been a fact of life. As Micah pointed out, "A man's enemies are the men of his own house." The ultimate solution is for the generations to finally be honest with each other and support each other in as many reasonable and valid ways as they can. Family relationships can sometimes be preserved only by disappointing unreasonable economic expectations.

CHAPTER 12

A WORD TO THE WEALTHY

*T*hey say that money is the root of all evil. Not so: it is also the flower, the leaves, and the stem. In fact, money has so many other functions that we sometimes lose sight of its primary, utilitarian purpose as a medium of exchange. It easily becomes the currency of emotional exchange. If we understand the many meanings of money, it becomes easier to maintain family relationships on a more dynamic level.

As one of my friends put it, "Money isn't everything, but it's a great way of communicating with your children." It's easy to express feelings through the giving and receiving of money. All sorts of emotions can be expressed: love, shame, envy, anger. Unfortunately, we sometimes substitute money for many of these emotions; many children of successful parents make this complaint. All too often, the pursuit of money replaces the necessary passion for life.

Many of the money problems of my generation were originated by the "Rockefeller syndrome." The Rockefellers had produced a barrage of propaganda promoting the idea that money did not buy happiness; the elder Rockefeller was constantly represented as handing out dimes to the grandchildren who washed his car. Real money was to be used to build churches and wipe out malaria; children presumably were not to waste money on. The Rockefeller family did everything possible to increase their wealth and perpetuate it, but used every device to hide it from our view. The whole concept was a useful one for providing me with many of my patients during the early years of my practice.

Some of my patients with the worst problems were the sons and daughters of wealthy families like the Rockefellers, who tried to teach their kids the value of money by not giving them any. Many of these unfortunate kids turned into psychopaths, doing things like stealing the family jewels. They saw their parents living on the high hog and became angry; they felt their parents were being hypocritical and cruel.

Most of my friends have problems with their adult children that frequently revolve around money. But, very often, these are very solvable. A wealthy lady friend was very troubled recently. She had given an old family television set to her son after buying herself a new one, and her daughter was enraged. The daughter claimed (and rightfully so, my friend said) that her brother was getting more of the old family possessions than she. My friend had recently been divorced and had moved into a smaller home; both children were grown and living on their own. She went on to explain that an unusual combination of events had led to this unequal distribution of old family possessions, although there had been no such original intention. In fact, she felt that she had more than compensated her daughter in other ways through direct financial support. But her daughter was still grieving over the missing television set and my friend felt guilty about it.

She was looking to me pathetically for any possible solution. I stared back at her and said, "So why don't you buy your daughter a new television set?" She looked startled and then started to laugh. She could well afford to do so, but it had never occurred to her. When she made the purchase, the ruckus subsided. On a subsequent date, I recited to her my famous family sermon, which goes as follows: "If a problem can be solved by the expenditure of money, and the money is available, then it's not a problem." My lady friend took my advice to her friends and returned to report that they had all been startled by my message of hope and became more relaxed with their children. I pass the sermon along to the reader. Be grateful if you can solve your problems that simply.

SERMONETTE

My generation of parents shared their sexual fantasies with their children more freely than they did their ample income. But it has never been possible to raise decent children in a wealthy atmosphere when they are denied money. It is truly hypocritical. Unless we are to sew all of our money into the mattress and never use it for anything, we must share it equally among us. There is no way people can have honest family relationships without sharing access to money as well as all other family assets.

Implicit in my assertion that many family problems can, and should, be solved with money is, of course, the assumption that the family is either prosperous or has some access to money through government aid, loans, TV, or winning the lottery. When a problem can't be solved with money, it falls into a more serious category. Most real problems, of course, are insoluble by money: chronic illness, stupidity, marital incompatibility, homosexuality, senility, schizophrenia. These are too serious to respond to such a simple solution. But there are many other problems that can indeed be solved with money.

At least one person to whom I was related by marriage took umbrage at my remarks about money and accused me of corrupting my family. Nothing is further from the truth. I am not saying that money buys happiness. I am simply saying that if some of our problems can be easily solved with money, why not be grateful—and use it?

CHAPTER 13

GRANDPARENTHOOD

"There are fathers who do not love their children; there is no grandfather who does not adore his grandson." Victor Hugo, *Les Miserables*

"Every generation revolts against its fathers and makes friends with its grandfathers." Lewis Mumford, *The Brown Decades*

*W*hen asked why he got along with his grandchildren so well, Maimonides is reputed to have replied, "Because they are the enemy of my enemy." This quote came to mind one afternoon when talking about being a grandparent with a woman I have known for many years. She and her husband are high achievers and proud of what they have done. We both have sensational granddaughters who were born within a few weeks of each other. But, as we talked, we both confessed to having similar feelings about our grandchildren, and similar grandparenting problems.

I complained very vehemently about my resentment that my granddaughter had recently grown up without even asking my permission—she had developed her own thoughts, feelings, prejudices. I was totally unprepared for her development into adulthood; she used to be so lovable, so compliant—now I faced an independent human being. I had already been through all that with my children, and it was hard to have to once more face that fact that little girls do not stay cute and adoring forever. Furthermore, I complained to my friend, I had reason to suspect that my granddaughter loved her parents as much as she did me. I considered this totally unacceptable. The least she could do was cause some family difficulty so that I could intervene to solve the problem, playing the role of the wise, heroic grandfather.

My friend listened to my tale of woe, laughed, and agreed that being a grandparent did have its difficulties. But then, as she pointed out, we were lucky—many people in our generation have no grandchildren at all, either because they didn't have children, or because their children didn't reproduce. Some people are grandparents only because one of their children married a divorced partner who already had children, making them accidental grandparents. Some were, but are no longer, grandparents: a divorced child may have lost custody of the children, and they have thus become token grandparents who are rarely, or never, seen by their grandchildren because of the hostility between the parents. Indeed, a whole new body of law is being developed to deal with the problems of grandparents who have lost access to their grandchildren.

A large number of grandparents see their grandchildren only on official occasions: Thanksgiving, Christmas, birthdays. And if the children are successful, that success is likely to mean that the grandparent has only limited contact with the grandchildren since the parents are apt to be highly mobile, constantly traveling on business or taking vacations in faraway places. It is usually true, moreover, that when the older generations meet with the rest of the family only on special family occasions and holidays the contact tends to be impersonal, especially as the grandchildren approach adulthood. The grandparents then become just an interesting curiosity to them.

These situations are often difficult for everyone involved, especially when the middle generation is having its own problems. In these uncertain times, they may not be able to finance a lifestyle like their parents had achieved, nor can they offer their own children the privileges they once took for granted when they were growing up. This circumstance puts the grandparents on the spot, making them go through incredibly complex gyrations of guilt, love, and responsibility while trying to maintain both financial and emotional harmony between all three generations.

A patient of mine, about thirty-five years old, told me that, although she seldom saw her grandmother, she and her sister remembered having wonderful times with her when they were young children. They both still had positive feelings about her and held her in high regard. I pointed out that her positive feelings went back to her own childhood, and asked her if she assumed that her grandmother also shared her nostalgia for the past—or might she instead feel rejected and alone because her granddaughters no longer visited her? Our emotions about grandparents usually reflect our nostalgic memories—pictures of the past that are no longer accurate, but have been distorted by a lack of significant new experiences. Youngsters retain fond memories of their grandpas and grandmas and assume the grandparents continue to feel the same way, even though they no longer see them.

There are, of course, other emotions between the generations that are less positive than sentimental nostalgia. One is the feelings grandparents have about their sons- or daughters-in-law. Many grandparents are afraid that they will try to take away, or restrict access to, their grandchildren. For instance, in a custody case some years ago, I was testifying for the wife, who was my patient. I wanted to help her. She was frightened and desperately wanted her children, but had few resources. I knew that her real adversary was the husband's father, who didn't want to lose his grandchildren. "I am the father of sons and have grandchildren," I told the court. "I know many fathers in the same position. We are all convinced that our daughters-in-law are not really capable of raising our grandchildren—the same grandchildren of whom we boast. We are sure she's not a good enough mother, yet somehow she has produced these absolutely miraculous offspring. My patient may be no more competent as a mother than any other daughter-in-law, but she loves her children and I believe that she should be given her chance, like the others." My patient was granted custody.

It's also usually true that if there's any trouble between grandparent and grandchild people automatically assume the older person is at fault. Take, for example, a commercial for a tranquilizer shown at a recent medical conference I attended. A grandmother was pictured involved in "meaningful contact" with her little granddaughter, teaching her to sew. An ugly spat arose between the two, and the announcer interrupted the scene for a message. He blamed the grandmother for losing control, and recommended she be given the tranquilizer in question to bring her emotions under control and help her get along with the little girl. Nobody mentions that the child's behavior was far from ideal, or that perhaps she'd been difficult, ill-mannered, or stupid, and deserved to be reprimanded.

This scenario is true to life. In every emotional confrontation between older people and the younger generations in our society, we always assign blame to the older person. This may be the reason that violence against senior citizens is escalating. The House Select Committee on Aging has estimated that more than a million elderly Americans each year are abused by relatives and loved ones physically, emotionally, and financially.

Grandparents presumably enjoy all the dividends of the love of their grandchildren with none of the responsibilities of parenthood. This is all very true, but the reverse side of the coin is the frequency with which the adult children flaunt their own children as superior examples of what good parenting is all about. Many adult children feel that their upbringing was seriously deficient, and they are going to prove to themselves and their elderly parents that they can do a much better job by being less permissive, less overprotective, and so forth, than their parents were. But these efforts very often fail. And nothing warms the heart of a grandparent more than to observe his children having the same problems that he had as a parent. It gives him a chance to confirm his suspicion that nobody knows all the answers and it gives the family an opportunity to enjoy their mistakes together—and to keep trying.

SERMONETTE

There is no question that being a grandparent is one of the great pleasures in life for the aging, and I would be the last to deny its value. Grandparenthood gives us the opportunity to, in a sense, relive our lives, correct old attitudes, develop new relationships with a younger age group, and undo the damage done in the past. But we cannot overlook the fact that any society that does not respect its children is not apt to honor its aged either. Thus, the alliance between the young and the old that seemed so natural to Maimonides is actually in jeopardy.

I would like to recommend that the very positive experiences shared by grandparent and grandchild be maintained in fact rather than in myth—it's unfortunate that most often I hear of these experiences in reminiscences rather than as current relationships. Most of the older people I talk to about their grandchildren are talking in the past, not in the now. And most grandchildren are still dreaming about Santa Claus and living in the past, and are disappointed, when they occasionally see their grandparents, to discover that they're not the same people they remembered. But this doesn't have to be the case. Anything that good should be maintained at any cost.

CHAPTER *14*

SOME PARADOXES OF WIDOWHOOD

*W*idows and widowers are an interesting group; I've been part
of that world for the past several years. The more widows that I've
gotten to know, the greater the surprises. In addition to having many
widows as friends, I have a reasonable number of surviving women
in my practice, and I have been privileged to serve as an executor
of the wills of some of my deceased friends. This has provoked
some unexpected reactions in me which I would like to share with
you.

The most surprising observation is that not all widows are pathetic and lonely. After the initial shock of bereavement, some for-
merly "happily married women" do quite well on their own. This
is not to say that they are necessarily happier (although some are),
just that they function better as unmarried women. Of course, we
have to allow for the debilitating effects of the prolonged illness of
their husbands, the shock of the husbands' death, and the structural
changes in their lives that come as a result.

But if we are to be truthful with ourselves, the fact that so many
widows do so well alone can tell us something about the nature of
some of the marriages of my generation. If so many women function
so well without their husbands, maybe being married was not such
a great experience for them. Our group expected to get married, did

marry, and tended to stay married. If the truth be known, many of these women had enormous unrealized capabilities which they perhaps, unwittingly, sacrificed for home, family, and stability; men were not expected to make any equivalent sacrifices. Women easily slid into dependent patterns and deferred using their independent judgments. Despite the fact that many of them were far superior to their husbands in intellect, aged better, and developed their minds more effectively, they continued to play inferior roles. Frequently the husbands deteriorated through the years, and some of the best husbands became impossible to live with. But it is hard for the widow to admit that she is happy to be relieved of her wifely burdens.

I don't think it is only true of my generation that most women tend to defer to men in the management of money, or in dealing with numbers in general. It is also true that the happier the marriage, the more the woman will tend to be willing to give in in order to avoid conflict. This is even more true if the man should happen to be competent, but not necessarily so.

It is only after the death of their husbands that women become aware of how much they have depended on their mates. They may lean on the executor, but he is no husband. Only in their unhappiness do they finally learn that they may be truly competent themselves. They may not like it, but it's a pleasure to see them spreading their wings, managing their own money, traveling by themselves, establishing new relationships on a more equitable basis.

Other widows, however, are convinced that they cannot make it on their own. They refuse to sharpen their minds, refuse to change, and may rush blindly into any new relationship, which usually turns out to be much worse than their marriage had been. Included in this group is the substantial number of women in my age group whom I categorize as "brutalized." A cruel marriage, economic oppression, and disappointing children (frequently addicted or psychopathic) bring these women to widowhood in a state of shock and mistrust. They have lost all trust in their own mental abilities, in relationships, and in the future. They are the victims of a traditional monogamy which was weakened by the rebellion of the 1960s and today's increasing longevity. They are frequently bright, attractive, and seemingly socially acceptable women, and yet they continue to function like remnants of a system which hopefully will rearrange itself with the liberation of women.

I have long felt that no woman should have to wait for her husband to die to learn to be a well-adjusted widow. It is a rare woman of my generation who ever had any conception of the family finances, practical arrangements for travel, or the techniques of earning a livelihood. I was constantly training my wife to be a widow. She would laugh at me, but I became frightened after a while at how well she could do without me. The risks were worth it, however, because I knew that some day she could take over if I should become incapacitated in any way. It is much easier for a woman to learn to be competent while her husband is still alive.

Given an equal financial status, I am always pleasantly surprised to observe how well many widows perform compared to widowers. They have networking skills, can usually cook for themselves, can manage their households, and can keep themselves clean and neat. It's a rare man who can do these things for himself. Men are salvaged by the imbalance in numbers; there is always some competent lonely woman who makes herself available to take care of him.

But life has its complications for even the most prosperous of widows. The women of my generation never earned the money themselves, and today they may be under continual pressure to share their largesse with their families, especially if they are less prosperous.

The wealthy widow and her suitors are in the newspapers almost daily. The problems of financial relationships become so complicated, the prenuptial arrangements so tacky, that many older widows prefer to remain unmarried and maintain separate residences with loved ones rather than try to resolve the problems. This money difficulty is separate from the unwillingness of most women to live through the nursing of an ailing man through a fatal illness—for a second or third time. In addition, the sexual problems of widows are enormous and few discussions in the literature are honest.

SERMONETTE

The years of widowhood are difficult for most women. Unfortunately, they are made even more difficult by the image of widowhood as a period of doom and gloom that is prevalent in our society. But, on the other hand, for many women it can become an opportunity for a new life. One of the advantages of the increased longevity and health of our society is that it offers an opportunity for multiple serial lives and marriages to the fortunate survivors. Those who are vital and courageous can, and should, rise to the opportunity. It may cause problems with their families, but nothing is for free.

CHAPTER 15

THE MALE SURVIVOR

*M*y family history is quite unusual and may give me a special point of view on male survivorship. My background is very male-oriented, and closely resembles my father's: each of us was separated from his mother at about eighteen years of age—my father because of his emigration from Europe, I because my mother died at the age forty-two; both of us made good marriages in our early twenties; we both survived our wives, each of whom died of cancer at the height of their powers; both my father, after my mother's death, and I after my wife's, had to reconstruct our personal and family lives without the benefit of adult female companionship, since neither of us had older sisters, aunts, mothers-in-law, or mistresses (my father had three unmarried brothers to comfort him; I had two adult sons and their families); both of us were in excellent health when we were bereaved, and in reasonably secure economic circumstances.

First my father, and then I, found that it's quite difficult to maintain the family unit intact when the significant woman for whom everybody has feelings, good or bad, is gone. Any hardworking man can have difficulty keeping his family together, but it's particularly difficult when the reconstructed family is all male and the sons' wives are not in a position to assume the responsibility for organizing the family network. For all practical purposes, even though good relationships often do exist between fathers and sons, the family will cease to be a family unless the father is a most unusual man and can become both a father and a mother to his children.

Some of my friends have commented that I became a more forthcoming and expressive man after I was widowed. I explained to them that I had always spoken quite openly, but only to my wife; she had always represented my point of view to them. After her death, I was, for the first time, representing myself to them directly; my spokeswoman was gone. But my thoughts had always sounded better when my wife paraphrased them. (In fact, I found that a number of people didn't seem to like me as much when I began to speak for myself.) My wife was my buffer, my interference; she was able to make me more socially acceptable. After she was gone, it became necessary for me to learn how to express my thoughts and my affection more directly. While this is a difficult adjustment for a father, particularly for those of my generation, it is well worth it—both for the father and for the family as a whole.

Another area of difficulty for the widowed father lies in the fact that our increasingly geriatric society has no precedents for handling intergenerational relationships between widowed father and competing sons without the mother there to act as the peacemaker. This competition can be in many areas: finances, status, sexuality. But if the father wants the family to survive the mother's death, he must learn to abdicate some of his power and reduce the competition with his sons. There is, of course, the geographical solution, in which the father simply retires from the competitive world, migrates to Florida, and becomes an absent elder statesman.

The tranquility created by a geographical cure is usually not disturbed unless the father presumes to remarry—which he is, these days, quite apt to do. The children might feel their father is being disloyal to them and to the memory of their mother. Just as problematic, however, especially if the bride is a younger woman, is the fact that the children just don't know how to cope with the reality that their elderly father remains an actively sexual being in their mother's absence.

The acceptance today of sex in old age can create some very difficult problems for widowers of my generation. Most of these men are simply not comfortable with the freedom of our times; they tend to feel anxious and confused when expected to ''perform'' by the women they may be dating after their wives' deaths.

This has a lot to do with our upbringing, of course. My father's generation was not perceived as sexual beyond the age of, perhaps, fifty. Older people then were supposedly capable only of platonic relationships. But the sexual revolution of the 1960s changed that perception. Nowadays we've gone to the other extreme—older men are supposed to remain vibrant forever, and the problems of sex in old age have become staple topics of television talk shows, sitcoms, and soap operas. But nobody seems to remember that my generation was already in its fifties when the revolution came along. It's unreasonable to think that we can conform to expectations that for most of us are not realistic.

SERMONETTE

It would seem possible for older men to survive the deaths of their wives on their own, but not really as part of a family—unless they learn to fulfill some of the functions in the family that their wives had performed: communicating more often and more directly with their children, becoming concerned for their health and day-to-day problems, and generally being more nurturing. Most men including myself find this difficult. This would not only improve the relationships between widowed fathers and their children, but could also better a widower's relationshps with the new women in his life, as well as bring him more up to date with today's society. For the one thing that we have learned is that older men, like their younger contemporaries, have to learn to live in a society where their behaviour is not determined by their anatomy.

CHAPTER 16

IS SEX ALWAYS NECESSARY?

"Age only matters when one is aging. Now that I have arrived at a great age, I might as well be 20." Pablo Picasso, at 80

*D*espite the increasing infirmities associated with growing older, a large segment of the older population remains in vigorous good health, and "the aging" now have to be distinguished from "the aged."

Many older people fully enjoy their later years, and even become liberated by growing older. For the first time they are unburdened of responsibility: they may no longer need to work, but freely choose to do so; older women are released from their childbearing functions and may feel freer than ever before to express their feelings honestly. In today's world, if one can manage to retain one's health (and many of us do), the later years can be a time of great personal freedom and opportunity. For many, it can be a period of explosive creativity, especially in the arts and literature, less so in the sciences. We have always had our Leonardos, Picassos, Tolstoys and Toscaninis, and now a whole new cycle of older people is learning to think and act creatively, some for the first time in their lives.

All of these opportunities for aging people, however, are at least partially determined by the degree of comfort or discomfort in their personal lives, that is, their state of health and the availability of creature comforts. The game is over if either is lost, for, as Cicero stated, "Old age is impossible to bear in extreme poverty, even if one is a philosopher."

As I stated before, the sexual revolution took place during the mature years of the present generation of older people. Most of us were in our fifties when it occurred, and our basic morality had been determined long before. During my early adult and married years not only did the adult period seem shorter (which it was), but the older years were much more reserved. The sexual life of the average person, certainly among married couples, seemed even shorter. Most couples were faithful to each other and apparently stopped (or so it seemed) having sex after the childbearing period. Freud is reputed to have stopped having sex at the age of forty-two, after the birth of his last child.

Forty years ago, most of my patients began to slow down as they grew older. Most of them expected to do so and, if it didn't happen, it was a pleasant surprise. Of course, their children never expected them to remain sexually active into their later years. In any event, whatever happened was a private matter, and the less said the better.

Whether their sexual life was really shorter, who can say? There were no population studies before Kinsey's in 1948. There were obvious exceptions to the usual norm, of course, and the phrase "dirty old man" seemed to encapsulate our prejudices. Flirtatious older women were considered eccentric or senile. I remember how my typist and my editor reacted when I wanted to include the chapter "Sex and Old Age" in my book *Paradoxes of Everyday Life*, which was published in 1953. They seemed to feel that it was in the worst possible taste. In the end, it didn't seem worth offending so many people, so I dropped the chapter. It was only a few years later that studies began to appear about the previously unrecognized sexual life of older people.

Of course, everybody knows that younger generations have always been embarrassed by the sexual life of their parents and elders.

Maybe they are now less offended, but I don't think that's really true, and we still live in a culture which equates youth with sex. Adult children certainly don't like to hear about the sexual activities of their widowed parents. The younger generation always feels that it has an exclusive option on the orgasm.

My first contact with this problem came at the end of World War II when some of the veterans began to return from overseas. A patient of mine, a successful young bank executive, typical of other young men in their thirties, had gone off to the war, leaving behind a lovely wife and two children. It had been a good marriage in which the sex had been satisfactory, although it was slowing down to the rate of once a week. By the standards of my practice at that time, they would be grandparents by the time they were fifty, and sex would then be a pleasant memory.

Within six months after the end of the war, the marriage was on the rocks. The soldier had had an affair with a Red Cross nurse while overseas and had enjoyed the excitement and frequency of a newfound sexual freedom. He tried to make the readjustment to his marriage, but his wife and he seemed to be on different wavelengths, and divorce followed very shortly. Changing sexual patterns were beginning to cause problems within the family.

I had another enlightening experience at about the same time. I received a phone call from a man who said he would like to consult with me—but only if I would promise not to laugh at him. When I acted surprised at such a request, he informed me that every other physician had embarrassed him by dismissing his problem as frivolous.

He was a sixty-two-year-old healthy, distinguished gentleman who had been treated with amused deference by all of the doctors with whom he had consulted about his sexual problem. It was obvious that his physicians had not expected him to be performing sexually. On the phone, I managed to reassure him that I would treat the problem with the proper respect. I was thirty years old at the time, and I must say that I seemed to share all the prejudices of my time.

When the patient told his story, it was apparent that he had a better understanding of himself than his physicians did: he had a sexual problem of psychological origin, totally unrelated to his age. He had been happily married to a woman he loved and to whom he had been faithful for over twenty-five years. He had been a widower for ten years, and had two grown sons who were now running his business. He was a pillar of the synagogue and led a cultivated life. Healthy and financially secure, he was now planning to remarry and retire. Unfortunately, he was impotent with the one woman he cared for and hoped to marry; but he was quite potent with the women with whom he was more casually involved. It was the classical problem of sacred versus profane love, and, within a short period of therapy, he responded quite well.

As he was leaving after his last visit, I couldn't resist asking him a question which had preoccupied me from the moment he came to the office. I had not fully comprehended the full nature and extent of the sexual activities of his age group (which was that of my father's) and expressed my wonderment at their freedom as contrasted to my own age group; we were only one step beyond Victorianism.

With his hand on the door, ready to leave, he seemed shocked by my surprise. "Don't you understand, doctor? All of the women I take out are beyond childbearing age. I date only beautiful women, usually grandmothers in their fifties, who are beyond their menopause. They are attractive women who cannot become pregnant, so why would they say no?"

This practical man predicted for me the coming of the sexual freedom of the 1960s with the discovery of oral contraceptives. The world would never be the same. If a woman could control her fertility, she lost a powerful deterrent to protect her virtue. The postmenopausal women in my patient's life didn't need oral contraceptives.

All of this has changed in the past thirty years. The sexual activities of older people have become much more visible. Serious academic studies at Duke University during the 1950s and 1960s confirmed that sexual activity was increasing among the older age group as people lived longer and stayed healthier. The press became flooded with articles on virility in old age, cheering us on. Several serious volumes appeared which encouraged older people not to forsake their capacities and newly-discovered opportunities. In the intervening years, the increasing lifespan, awakened sexual freedom, new vitamins, new plastic surgery, the increasing divorce rate among the elderly, and the geriatric athletic marathon all led to much media publicity about sexual activity in old age.

One celebrity after another has written books and magazine articles describing his or her amorous adventures, and David Brown, husband of Helen Gurley Brown, recently recommended that every older man should have a few girlfriends in addition to his marriage. But how much relevance does Elizabeth Taylor's—or any celebrity's—sex life have for the average man or woman? Nobody notes how inapplicable these special opportunities are for the average older man and woman who is not a millionaire, a star, or a producer of movies. For every person who is encouraged by these stories, a hundred others are frightened off.

Put simply, sex is now considered a perpetual gift to mankind; it is never supposed to wither or disappear. An article in the *New York Times* stated that 38 percent of the population believed that sex goes on forever. That's quite a switch in a few years.

But all this media hype creates unrealistic expectations in both sexes. It places older women under undue stress to be provocative, sexy, and flirtatious, and challenges most men beyond their own perceived capacity. It is my experience that any widow who is bold enough to announce in advance that she expects her boyfriend to be super-potent seldom gets taken out; her attitude (fueled by the media) raises expectations to the point where the unusual is considered the norm. In fact, the problems of sex in old age are similar to the problems of adolescence forty years ago: fears of performance on the part of the man, the insecurities of feeling inadequate on the part of the woman.

But sex is not always available to everyone in old age, as this media blitz might lead us to believe. And the often unrealistic expectation that we should be sexually active until we die makes many aging people feel inadequate and isolated. For this and many other reasons, many older people actually avoid sexual activity.

Most of the proponents of active sex in the older age group hate to mention the fact that of the twelve million people over fifty, only two million are men. These figures are further complicated by the fact that older men find it easier than women to leave their age group to find a partner, and all studies indicate that sexual activity is directly proportional to the availability of partners. Age is secondary.

But not only is there a shortage of available elderly men, women's orgastic capacity is escalating while men's is declining. As women are becoming more sexually functional, men are becoming less so, and this is bound to create problems. In order for sex to be functional in old age, men have to give up any pretense of sexual dominance, especially since women are now so easily orgastic, while men are struggling to maintain an erection. This is difficult for people of my generation to accept.

In addition to these difficulties, in old age women tend to lubricate less and men tend to take longer to reach a full erection (although these factors don't necessarily have to affect performance). But the true problem is lack of a partner, not age. For women today, however, there are plenty of new books which will teach them how to masturbate, although this may still be a taboo subject to those of my generation.

A problem associated specifically with unmarried sexual contact in later life is the guilt generated when the man withdraws from a relationship; since he is so difficult to replace, casual sex is almost unthinkable. Older women are ready to give up sex rather than face the disappointments of uncommitted relationships. For the older woman, sexual contact is unthinkable without some commitment. Marriage is usually secondary to loyalty within the relationship; in fact, many older, self-sufficient women would prefer not to take the risk of marriage again.

It may no longer be possible for older people to admit to themselves, and certainly not to the outside world, that they are no longer interested in sex. It is also harder now to admit that'they are incapable of having sex, unless they can blame it on diabetes or anti-hypertensive drugs. There are a lot of older people who are ashamed, embarrassed, and angry at each other because they have lost interest in sex, or can no longer function sexually. They feel that they should be part of the sexual revolution, and, out of fear and inadequacy, they stop being tender, often giving up on valid relationships.

This remarkable reversal has led to as much guilt about failure in old age as we used to see in adolescents in the old days. I have been the confidant of many men, professionally as well as personally, who have avoided commitment in their later years because they feel that they cannot keep up with the sexual demands presented by the media to our increasingly geriatric society. Disappointed, women usually don't realize what is happening, and escalate the problem by acting increasingly provocative.

SERMONETTE

Few elderly people today are willing to admit that perhaps they don't have to conform to today's concept of never-ending sexuality. In the old days, this was an acceptable thing to do, but not in today's climate of hype. But the fact is that many marriages are sexless and still serve a meaningful function for the participants. Nobody is recommending it as a way of life, but we do have to confront the fact that family life goes beyond sexual stimulation. People—married or unmarried—need one another for a variety of reasons: companionship, intellectual stimulation, financial support, and endless other pleasures. In the old days, couples could stay together after the first passions had subsided without feeling inadequate. This should still be possible.

The old image we grew up with of a quiet, sexless old age was obviously false, but the new image is perhaps even more ridiculous. Life would be simpler if older people could freely reach their own conclusions on the combination that would best suit them of love, companionship, touching, tenderness, and sexual fulfillment.

CHAPTER 17

SURVIVING OUR LOSSES IN OLD AGE

*O*ld age is not for sissies. It's painful to keep on living as our friends and families die or drift away. Those who cannot handle the losses that are part of growing older are knocked out early in the game. Successful survivors know how to become detached from their losses in order to handle the ensuing depression and loneliness. It's a wonder how many older people do manage to survive and function effectively.

The capacity to deal with loss may well be the most important single factor in the maintenance of good mental health. Life is a process of growth and a series of losses. The child who cannot handle loss of parental support, the widower who cannot face life alone, the divorced wife who can never forgive her husband for the other woman, the businessman who cannot adjust his lifestyle to a lowered income all can become chronically depressed.

Emotionally mature people build on past experience, establish new relationships that are sometimes even better than those they lost, and continue to lead productive lives in the face of loss. They can forget the past and get on with their lives; they can lose their treasures, survive irretrievable losses, and still renew themselves.

What is their secret? They've probably had good relationships in the past that ended without excessive guilt. They are probably not unusually dependent people, and feel capable of surviving on their own if necessary. Loneliness is not a threat to them. Most importantly, they know who they are. Almost invariably, they have successfully survived losses when they were young. They understand the transitory nature of life and accept the fact that nothing is forever.

We all have to be prepared for the possibility that our lives can change at any moment. But older people cannot take anything for granted; from one day to the next, our support systems—friends, colleagues,. accountants, shoemakers, secretaries—may be gone. Not to mention our status, our money, our teeth, and our bladder control.

Loss at any age brings the family and intergenerational loyalties into true perspective. A little boy needs his mother when he loses his puppy, an adolescent needs the support of his parents when he is stood up on an important date, an elderly widower needs his sons, daughters, and friends when his wife dies—we all need the love and understanding of our families during difficult periods in our lives.

The traditional family had a large enough brood to allow for the losses of any one member. But today when we face losses our family of origin may not be able to provide this support—either due to emotional conflicts or because it is no longer in existence. In this event people, particularly the elderly, can and should build new families, or support systems. It may sound cold, but with enough imagination it is possible to replace almost any loss with a new interest, activity, or person. But, of course, things are much easier when one's family is there as a safety net.

When losses are truly devastating, such as a combination of loss of earning capacity, loss of health, and loss of spouse or family, then a benign social service network becomes the only solution for the elderly survivor.

SERMONETTE

We all lose significant relationships throughout our lives: a parent, a spouse, a close friend, a child. The ability to survive the loss and continue to function without excessive grief, depression, or anxiety is what separates the men from the boys, the women from the girls.

The ability to hold on to oneself in the face of loss, to replace relationships, to think things through and maintain one's integrity as a person, these are the conditions for sustained life and continuity in old age. Otherwise, we might as well throw ourselves into the grave along with our spouses. Ultimately, all creativity is a way of replacing our losses. The biology of man is very cruel, and our consciousness of the evanescence of life is the price we pay for being human.

Family relationships offer all of us, particularly the aged, the one great hope for the replacement of our losses, big and small. Without this support, or an adequate replacement, few of us can survive. Only the ability to establish a new support system makes it possible for the elderly person to deal with the many losses of advancing age.

CHAPTER 18

OLD FRIENDS, NEW FRIENDS, AND LONELINESS

*L*oneliness is the terror which frightens us all. The family unit (marriage, ongoing relationships with siblings, the emotional attachments of the older generation to their offspring) is our protection against isolation and the anxiety which accompanies it. With no villains to accuse, the universal fragmentation continues, affecting children as much as parents. Any one person may be forced to seek other alternatives, new relationships, new families.

The worst possible scenario for an older person is the loss of a spouse. The painful loss of this most intimate relationship creates a deep fear of the imminent dissolution of the family, as well as a desperate sense of loneliness. This can be a horrifying experience.

The shocking impact of the spouse's death, the circumstances of his dying, the funeral, the rush of family and friends to the side of the bereaved are all a stressful, though necessary, part of the grieving process. But once the funeral is over life alone becomes very difficult; one's children (if they are old enough), friends, and family all return to their homes, and the survivor must rebuild a life by himself, unwillingly assuming the entirely new role of "single older person."

There seem to be more older widows than widowers and, frequently being less sophisticated in the area of finances, they seem to become less acceptable among the married couples they once socialized with along with their husbands. Widowed men, on the other hand, are better able to pursue new heterosexual relationships and maintain control of their finances. Yet, emotionally, they seem to fare worse than widows.

But togetherness is not always a blessing, and there are occasional survivors who are actually relieved to be left alone when someone in their family dies. For them, the family relationships were an emotional burden from the beginning. Many widows and widowers are determined never to marry again. And many adult children are relieved when they are forced to strike out on their own. There are always people, like those mentioned above, who are capable of maintaining their equilibrium without, at least temporarily, an ongoing relationship. But most people do experience deep feelings of loneliness when on their own.

Whatever the reason for loneliness, especially in old age, the problem is compounded by isolation, especially when children and other family members become less and less available: many older members of the family may have died; some may have moved to greener pastures, like the Sun Belt or various retirement communities; adult children may have become estranged over family disputes.

For most older people, there is a great need to live in familiar surroundings, preferably with old friends and family, but that's not always possible. Some people have no choice but to face new environments, new faces. This problem concerns many governmental agencies and private concern groups, who seek to establish appropriate new settings for the elderly. But the availability of new faces in new settings is not necessarily a solution for many people; we all know that it's possible to be lonely even when surrounded by people.

This sense of isolation is not unique to older people, of course: what is more devastating than an orphaned child? It seems that loneliness and isolation is most threatening to the very young and to the old.

Very few people have not known some form of loneliness at

some point during their lifetime: we often forget that many of our parents came to this country in their teens to live in a foreign culture without any money, very few friends, and no fluency in the new language; our children have known loneliness too, when going off to college, or when going off to war; and many of us know people who have survived the loneliness that comes from constant moving about during the childhood years, making it impossible to establish meaningful, lasting relationships. It's easy to say that relationships are not forever and that people come and go for a variety of reasons, but loss is still a very difficult experience for us all.

Losing human connections is a process which can occur at any age, at any time. The loss of the capacity to relate to other people usually precedes the development of loneliness; it is rare for anybody to become lonely unless the process of physical isolation and incipient depression has already begun. The good news is that the ability to reverse this process is always possible.

It would seem that the successful resolution of most forms of loneliness is almost invariably based on the person's capacity to relate to new people. After all, even though one cannot guarantee that old friends and family will always be around, new relationships are always available.

A fair number of older people seem to isolate because they are deluded into believing that only their old friends are real, intrinsically essential to their survival. Old childhood friends, departed spouses, children who are no longer accessible, all of these people are invested with an aura of unique closeness which may be quite unrelated to the actual experience.

But our old relationships may not have been as ideal as we make them out to be once they are gone. I have seen too many boring college reunions, too many pathetic Thanksgiving family gatherings, too many sad country club evenings to believe that old relationships are a guarantee of conviviality or genuine interchange of feelings or ideas. This glamorization of the past, and the depression that goes with it, is bad enough. But what is worse is that it prevents people from reaching out to fresh sources of support: new friends.

The unwillingness or inability to make new friends to replace old or estranged ones can be very harmful to anyone's emotional well-being, but it's particularly dangerous for the elderly. Don't get me wrong; I'm not saying we should discard all of our current relationships in favor of completely new ones. We all need and want a few comfortable relationships in a network where we can relax—most commonly in a marriage—among a selected handful of special people. This is to be understood. I am alluding to the number of older people who systematically socialize only with old friends. When those old friends die or move away, these people are left helpless and denuded, having to reorganize their lives without support. In other words, when something unforeseen happens, they are unprepared to reorganize their social existence; they bemoan their fate and sink into depression. Just as every individual relationship has to be nurtured through the years, so a body of new relationships has to be developed. This is hard to do if old friends have a lock on loyalty.

Actually, I think many old friends are bored with one another, but hang around because it's effortless and unchallenging. Since most people are lazy when it comes to trying new things, it's easier to settle for familiarity. But the price is high when the crunch comes and the old friends disappear. The anger, the disenchantment, and the inability to make new friends is devastating. What is even worse is that many people denigrate their new friends, even when they do make some. They surround themselves with a phony nostalgia which is delusional and only serves to offend and repel their new friends.

I've always found the prospect of making new friends a very attractive one; we expect less from them, but sometimes are pleasantly surprised. My own personal experience has convinced me that the sources of help available to us in every area—professional as well as personal—are totally unpredictable. I have been repeatedly astounded by the generosity of people I barely knew, just as I have been disappointed in relationships which I had nurtured for almost a lifetime.

It is also my experience that some of the most exciting people I know tend to be the ones I have met most recently: the exploration of new ideas, new patterns of living, learning how they earn a livelihood, how they take vacations, stretches the mind into new areas. Another advantage of making new friends is that there are so many more of them, and they are always available if we take the trouble to look. There are many surprises, no old grudges, no false expectations. Of course, sometimes it does take considerable effort.

Senility is in the mind, and snobbery about old friends is the ultimate senility—which frequently begins early in life. Many people never leave the atmosphere in which they grow. Whether it be the *shtetl* in Poland or the WASP boarding school, they are locked in forever to their own misfortune, for not growing is the ultimate death.

SERMONETTE

Loneliness is not an incurable disease—it is always reversible. There are few human conditions that are so easily remedied.

When we are born, we are presented with a set of relationships. But soon we learn that life is filled with loss and replacement. Unless we are prepared to build new relationships and let go of old ones, we will too often find ourselves in lonely, sometimes even desperate, situations.

CHAPTER *19*

TIME OUT: THE REWARDS OF BEING ALONE

About twenty years ago, at a New Year's Eve party, I was conversing with a lady I had known for some years. She was about sixty years old, and I knew that her marriage was on very shaky ground. We were all acting decorously for the occasion, kissing at the stroke of midnight and wishing one another well on the coming year. Later that evening, the lady and I got to speaking about loneliness. It was a very inappropriate occasion for such a serious discussion, and I would like to believe that it was she who brought up the subject. Answering her questions in my usual matter-of-fact, parlor-room-psychiatrist manner, I suggested: "Isn't unhappiness worse than loneliness?" She took sharp issue with me. "But Milton, you have never experienced loneliness in your life. Besides, you don't understand what loneliness means to an older woman. Men never do understand what it means to be alone, or even worse, to be rejected." I rapidly backed away, sensing that I had better avoid any further discussion because of both the occasion and the tenuous nature of her marriage. The waters were getting too deep for a New Year's Eve conversation.

Two weeks later, I heard that the husband had left my friend for another woman and that she had committed suicide by an overdose of sleeping pills. It was obvious that she had made her choice:

loneliness, especially when coupled with rejection, was worse than being unhappy. I often think about my New Year's Eve encounter with that sad woman, especially when I have to deal with patients (particularly older ones) who cannot tolerate being alone, and the stupid things they do, or try to do, in order to avoid it. I know, and they know, that their problems could be solved if they could only tolerate a brief, though lonely, transitional period.

Many parents, as well as their adult children, will have to make the same choices as my unhappy friend. They will pay any price rather than being left alone or being rejected. I may be oversimplifying complex problems, but the fact remains that many people have to make the choice between either being alone or being in unhappy situations many times during their lifetime.

The inability to be alone causes frightened people to make silly marriages with catastrophic results, older parents to make poorly advised financial arrangements with their children in order to guarantee continuing contact, and younger people to remain under family protection forever, fearful of striking out on their own. But those who can tolerate temporary isolation will have many more happy choices later.

Under normal circumstances, people willingly pay a reasonable emotional price for the companionship of other people or for belonging to a group. Nobody can relate to other people without adjusting somewhat to the other person's needs: no child finds his way into a school clique, no golfer joins a foursome, no man marries a lady without tuning in to the others' needs. This is the small sacrifice we must all make in order to avoid isolation, and it is a price that is well worth paying, because it is usually balanced by what we get in return. For most people, this is no problem.

But some people seem willing to pay an exorbitant price in exchange for very little or no return at all: their marital partner may be cruel and inhuman, they may have to swallow their pride in order to be accepted by the inner circle, their employer may treat them in a humiliating fashion. These people are too afraid of being alone to protest these abuses.

This becomes a particularly serious problem for many people

during the critical times in their lives: What price should a woman pay to hold on to her husband? What price should a son-in-law pay to work for his tyrannical father-in-law? What price should an outsider pay to belong to an insipid inner circle at the beach club? What price should parents pay to maintain the family intact?

Over and over again, I have to deal with those who suffer the worst kinds of indignities because they cannot face loneliness. Very creative, very intelligent people will sometimes sacrifice their personal fulfillment in order to avoid being alone. But the ability to survive temporary unhappiness is frequently necessary in order to reorganize one's life or to be creative. Many important activities—like thinking or writing a novel—demand being alone for a finite period of time. When we are younger, we have to be capable of being alone at least some of the time in order to live a creative or productive life. When we are older, there should be a way to continue to lead a fulfilling life without becoming hostage to our need to be with others.

From the Talmud, from the TV evangelist, from almost every psychoanalytic author, we get instructions to be part of a "loving world." And for many people the need for periods of solitude is necessary to rearrange the mind and to venture forth again into the world of friends, love, and commitment. Shyness and the need to be alone are now considered genetically determined in children, and are also a part of the creative processes of great artists like Kafka, Michelangelo, and Sir Isaac Newton.

It is creative writers who have perhaps the greatest need for solitude, but they are very special cases, for obvious reasons. Many writers not only learn to tolerate solitude, creating great works, but also learn to rejoice in it: "The happiest of all lives is a busy solitude," Voltaire wrote in a letter to Frederick the Great; "Whoever is delighted in solitude is either a wild beast or a god," Francis Bacon wrote in *Of Friendship*; "The strongest man in the world is he who stands alone," Henrik Ibsen commented in *An Enemy of the People*.

In recent years there has been a pendulum swing against the "togetherness" of the 1960s and 1970s. Solitary time is increasingly recognized as indispensable to the individual and his family. We simply cannot be continuously relating to one another, loving one another, exchanging witty remarks.

Of course, it has always been easier and more acceptable for a man to be alone, less so for women because of their caring and networking needs: they interact more with one another and share of themselves more than men, who have never even learned how to take care of themselves.

Sometimes I wonder if we don't overwhelm our children with the need to be too social and overexpressive. Togetherness can become a burden for all of us. Perhaps sleeping is our way of being alone with ourselves while preparing for the next day's burdens.

SERMONETTE

No family can remain in harmony if everyone has the need to be in continuous contact with one another. Members of the family need to be alone, to rest, to recharge their batteries, to cleanse their souls. The capacity to be happy while being alone should not be interpreted as a negative thing; the person who can find some companionship within himself is eventually a more effective family member and a happier, more creative human being.

CHAPTER *20*

SIBLINGS AGAIN

I have noticed in recent years that siblings often grow closer to one another as they get older. After years of rivalry, and even estrangement, they tend to reestablish some meaningful contact in their old age. It is of some interest that the one consistent factor associated with good emotional health in old age is the experience of having had good sibling relationships in childhood.

Social circumstances may contribute to this need in our later years to reestablish sibling relationships. The growing instability of marriage as a lifelong commitment leads brothers and sisters, as they become separated from their spouses, to gravitate toward one another. This instability may result from the death of a spouse, divorce, or the often exhausting stresses of a new marriage. The commonality of a shared childhood and parents becomes an important bond as the marriage license becomes less available or attractive. Familiarity and common history make the transition easier when one wants to leave one's spouse, or even one's children. The bonds of matrimony are thus replaced by blood relationships.

Another reason for reconciliation between elderly siblings is the fragility of family life today. They find it easier to relate to people of their own generation. Siblings try to reestablish relationships with one another to ease their feelings of isolation and pain.

Yet another factor in the importance of sibling relationships in old age is that many older people tend to move to retirement

89

communities. It's often a difficult transition for them, but it becomes easier when a familiar person already lives there. So, many try to move to places where their siblings are already living.

The increasing attention being paid to sexuality among the aged adds a lot of stress to the process of initiation of new relationships in old age. Many older people still retain the sexual credo of their youth and remain conservative and shy when it comes to their sexuality. Living with siblings helps them avoid the conflicts that can arise in this area. Since they are not alone, they feel less of a need to look for companionship that can lead to intimacy. The fact is that many older people are only too happy to avoid the complexity of new intimacies. Rekindling an older relationship with an established pattern of indifference may seem safer and much more preferable.

Various family matters can also bring siblings back together in their late years. These can include estate problems, deaths in the family, the distribution of inheritances, and the problems of caring for elderly parents. All of these often force siblings to deal with one another, and many of them choose to maintain the contact. And the great increase in interest in genetic disorders, national origin, family traditions, and ethnicity frequently draw brothers and sisters into renewed contact with one another as well. In my own family, the transfer of old family photographs to videotape has greatly increased our communications with one another.

Whatever the causes, the improving of sibling relationships aids family cohesiveness and is frequently associated with the revival of the family spirit.

SERMONETTE

It's easier to let go of resentments and mend fences with our siblings during old age. Many childhood problems begin to look insignificant after surviving the traumas of bad marriages, divorce, widowhood, or difficulties with our children. Siblings begin to forgive one another, look back on their early rivalries with amusement, and sometimes even realize that they were only pawns in the general family struggle.

When it comes to relationships between siblings, it's better late than never. Siblings who seem to develop an irrevocable dislike for one another that goes back many years nevertheless frequently find an affinity for one another in their later years. Drawn together by fortuitous circumstances, their reunion often provokes a welcome reawakening of many long-lost feelings toward one another and other members of their families. They can see their much loved parents, uncles, cousins reflected in their siblings' faces. And they can't figure out why they ever drifted apart.

CHAPTER *21*

ON DECLARING ONESELF DEAD

*I*t's wonderful when the parents maintain their position by great individual creative efforts, but it seems to me that part of the dignity of old age lies in the parents' recognition of their own limitations and their willingness to give the younger generation a chance at the limelight. It is possible to stop competing and still have a good old age.

Growing older is different from growing up, but both generations have to be aware of what's involved. Older parents are wise; they have a lifetime of experience to share with the younger generations. Why don't they share of this largesse with their families? The reason is simple: they often offer it, but younger people don't want it; they are too busy to hear any words of wisdom from their elders, no matter how much they love them. Adult children tend to ask for help only when it has direct practical value: babysitting or financial assistance, for instance. In fact, it's been my experience that it is easier for the younger generation to give advice than to receive it. This is interpreted by the aged as rejection, but it's only another manifestation of the computer age.

One alternative for the single older parent is to give up on his family and seek new pleasures in relationships with the opposite sex. This has its own problems, however. Everybody knows that it's a man's world because there are so few of them compared to the excess of unattached ladies. A good man can bring a lot of happiness to the world about him, but if the relationship goes beyond casual companionship, the men may feel that, due to the vulnerability of many older women, they are being pressured into a commitment they may not want or be ready for. Another factor is that most older men do more damage than good to the older women they date by becoming frightened off by sexual expectations which they fear they cannot live up to. On the other hand, most older women don't want to take care of incompetent, failing older men; they've usually been through it once already. The older man can always skip a generation and seek out the companionship of women in his children's age group. But this presents other problems and usually enrages everybody about him, especially his family and every woman who ever knew his wife.

So, forming romantic attachments to replace the emptiness of not having good family relationships is not always the answer. It may be a pleasant alternative temporarily, but it's an option that fails to address the problem that an elderly person's life is winding down, that his achievements are behind him, and that most people, including his own family, are beginning to consider him a burden.

But I have come up with another alternative which I find most useful: Why couldn't the older person simply declare himself dead? (Only to himself, of course.) The concept of life after death has always been an appealing one, so why can't he behave as if he were a visitor who has received special dispensation to return to earth for a short period of time? Everybody dreams he can return to the scene of his crimes and see his old world as an observer: he can discover how his children eventually turned out, how the Chinese solved their political problems—and he doesn't have to worry about dying, because, in his own mind, he already *is* dead. This concept can free us from a lot of the stress in our lives.

Thornton Wilder's "Our Town" and many T.V. sitcoms (like "Topper") have used the device of coming back after death, and it is obviously a good one. Why can't ordinary older citizens enjoy this privilege? They won't have to play phony games, they won't have to rule the world, they won't have to accomplish anything—and they can do lots of nice things for everybody (often by distributing their assets among them) without caring about the results. They can stop being grumpy, and if people look through them and act as if they don't exist, it's understandable to them—after all, they're dead, aren't they?

What a wonderful opportunity to balance the books, to correct the errors of an ignorant or impetuous past! Think of all the omissions committed, especially against his children, that he can now correct. Think of all the niceties he had begrudged his wife which he can now make up for by bestowing privileges on underprivileged female survivors. If necessary, he can even change his social fabric and start a new life. Most people who move to retirement communities are doing just that, without admitting to the world that they are turning their backs on the past and beginning a new life with their contemporaries.

When should an elderly person consider declaring himself dead? It's really quite arbitrary; it's up to him: perhaps when his wife dies, when his children treat him like a nuisance, when he loses his job, when he reaches the age of seventy-two, when he's tired of responsibility—it really doesn't matter. Once he does so, however, he psychologically becomes a free agent responsible only to himself. Having accomplished this great feat, he can still enjoy himself, he can be a participant observer, but, most importantly, he can simply walk away from unpleasantness. Possessions, status symbols, popularity all become less important.

Most older people spend much of their time worrying about their health and agonizing over the fear of dying anyway. Declaring themselves dead gives them the opportunity to stop torturing themselves because they have given up the battle for survival, having decided to live on borrowed time. It is also easier, when necessary, to become a public charge after declaring yourself dead. Things just don't matter as much.

How will this decision affect an older person's physical health? I believe it must prolong his life, because there is no question that indifference is the ultimate answer to many of our most painful and even unsolvable problems. The rages and frustrations of old age are dangerous to our health.

If heaven is such a wonderful place, why not try to create some of it here, in the real world? There is always time for actual physical death at the proper time—and it is much less threatening the second time around. Real death becomes easier to accept when the awareness of it is first accepted and then forgotten.

Interesting things happen to an older person's family and friends when he declares himself dead and seems to care less about their actions or reactions to him. They become concerned, perhaps even developing feelings of guilt, once they are aware that he is no longer depending on them. They may consider him depressed or going through some unexplained crisis. It always helps to jar them into paying attention.

SERMONETTE

The fear of death and of being alone in our old age has always caused untold misery in every society. When our families are not available to us for the support we need during this difficult time, we each must find some other way of living what remains of our lives in the most productive and fulfilling way possible. Punishing the family or making them feel guilty for neglecting us is not the answer. With a little bit of imagination, it is possible to stay alive while at the same time becoming a benign nonparticipant who is able to walk away from feelings of rejection. Playing dead simply means giving up power and looking for heaven on earth.

CHAPTER 22

POWER AND SURRENDER IN OLD AGE

*L*oss of power and status is one of the things the elderly fear most. Their power may be physical or mental, actual or fantasied, economic or personal—but whatever it is, the prospect of losing it worries every senior citizen. In our culture, to not have power implies worthlessness; its loss lowers our self-esteem and raises our level of anxiety. Our image of ourselves in relation to family, business, and social groups depends on our perceptions of where we fit in, our place in the hierarchy of power. Consequently, the reluctance to relinquish power and the fear of becoming inconsequential are serious problems for the aging.

Power struggles between the older and younger generations fill our literature, from the Bible to the *Village Voice*. These struggles are an unending source of unhappiness, greed, and political upheaval. On the other hand, the willingness to share our power with other generations in our family, whether by parents or children, is the essence of good family relationships.

Western philosophers like Machiavelli, Bergson, and Schopenhauer all agree on the importance of power, will, and *elan vital*.

Almost all human activities involve various forms of power: sometimes it's subtle, sensual, and seductive, other times it's violent, physical, and life-threatening. But in whatever form, everybody seems to love power. To some, the sense of being powerful is almost as good as a cocaine high. Friedrich Nietzsche observed: "Wherever I found a living creature, there I found the will to power." Many agree with him so deeply they feel they are dying when they lose their power. Call it "status" or "vitality"; it's all the same.

In primitive societies, power gave men access to the most desirable women, keeping the better (or more aggressive) genetic material alive. It also helped us to survive all kinds of natural enemies, including those within our own species. Thus, the struggle for power does make a lot of biological sense on a personal as well as a species level. It can teach a child how to deal with aggression, how to master his own world. It is a necessary tool for survival. The problem is that the power that served such a useful purpose for most of our lives turns into, when misused, one of the more foolish vanities of old age. Power for power's sake is counterproductive and serves almost no legitimate function for the elderly.

But most people hate to lose the feeling of power, and almost nobody seems to be willing to give it up, particularly in old age. Even in religion (except for a few fanatics in the Far East) power is rarely given up voluntarily: when Buddha gave up his temporal powers to form a new religion, he was actually seeking a new kind of power.

Many of the struggles between the generations revolve around the unwillingness of the older generation to pass the baton on to the younger one. But a few wise men have learned that it's better to give it up than to wait until it is forcibly taken from you.

Sometimes I wonder if power has any relationship to survival; if the more powerful don't end up as the first casualties (or the first criminals) in the struggle for survival. Too frequently, power results in extra risk. There is no question that tough people, such as professional football players or laborers, have a shorter lifespan than their more cowardly compatriots. And many recent medical studies indicate that individuals who cannot reduce their striving for power, who continue being aggressive and cannot turn off their desire for control, have a shorter lifespan.

In general, power today is beginning to seem somehow obsolete, pretentious, phony. One begins to wonder if compromise—or even withdrawal—isn't the more appropriate course in most situations. Is intelligence a valid form of power? or is physical violence the ultimate power? Since, in our old age, we no longer have physical power, perhaps we can learn to rely on our knowledge and intelligence as valid, alternative sources of power. It's paradoxical that, in a society that does not value intellect very highly, the loss of intellectual power becomes so meaningful in our later years: even those who have done nothing to develop their minds are afraid of losing it.

And how important is power in today's society? Was Machiavelli correct when he stated that the love of power is the love of ourselves? Do we actually have to live in a world in which it is more important to be feared than to be loved? Personally, I prefer the words of Lord Acton: "Power tends to corrupt; absolute power corrupts absolutely." How prophetic this Victorian gentleman was! The twentieth century has made a horror show of the exercise of power—what can we expect will happen in the twenty-first?

The problem with power is that it is so transitory. Power is never forever: the dictator is deposed, potentates die, sultans become impotent and look foolish to the harem, our parents grow old and weak as we grow stronger. Even worse, however, is that nobody ever seems to give up power willingly: the sultan castrates the males to maintain his illusion of sexual exclusivity; the egomaniac eventually becomes paranoid, for, inevitably, the next successor is always waiting in the wings; the elderly head of a family threatens his successors and potential heirs with disinheritance in order to keep them from questioning his authority.

The need to be powerful is a terrible curse. Every power lives in terror of losing his authority: a dictator slowly goes mad as he escalates his brutality in order to maintain his image. And there is nothing worse than believing your own press agents. The Pharaohs could not give up their power, assumed immortality in *The Book of the Dead*, and buried their treasures in the pyramids, hoping that nobody would catch up with them.

And who really enjoys power, anyway? Its possessors always seem so miserable and tense to me. I think that many American presidents seem relieved to give up their power when forced to do so by the Constitution.

In my view, the time has come for the older generation to give up power; like cigarettes, it's bad for the health. All power plays should now have to be smoked with tobacco substitutes; the illusion of power must perhaps replace its actuality.

Too many older people tend to feel pathetic and useless when they sense a loss of power or status—within their family, in their place of employment, in their relationship with their wives. But the loss of power is not a disease; it should instead be a welcome sign of maturity. The passing on of power to others may be the ultimate form of maturity. And there is nothing more ridiculous than an older citizen (male or female) preening himself, unaware of the decline of his powers. "Every hero becomes a bore at last," Emerson wrote in *Uses of Great Men*.

SERMONETTE

The exercise of power is necessary to run any organization, family, or political group. But as people live longer it becomes necessary to give up power earlier in life. It is very possible that many multigenerational families are destroyed when the elderly try to hold on to their power for too long.

But, of course, it can be extremely difficult for any of us to abdicate, to accept our limitations in old age. It is often too much for any one person to handle to retire, get old, begin to fail physically, and lose power and status—all at the same time.

But I offer an alternative: What about authority without power? Is this possible? I would think so; creativity, wisdom, enduring love, respect, cooperation, all carry a certain authority which never really dies and which doesn't cause insanity or paranoia. And a powerless old age can be quite productive if one's power is willingly surrendered while one is youthful and vigorous and at the height of one's competence. Since we will all lose power eventually, why not give it up voluntarily, before it has sown the seeds of resentment—and even hatred—within the family?

CHAPTER 23

WILL THE REAL ADULT PLEASE STAND UP?

*O*ne of the problems of living in a multigenerational world is deciding who plays the adult when most family members are grown up and authority is based on factors other than age. Are we all—parents and children—considered equally adult when our parents grow old? At what age should a father or mother stop acting "parental"? Once a child becomes a parent—or even a grandparent—should he still be considered a child in the eyes of his parents?

Other questions arise: How and when should older parents allow themselves to be taken care of by their adult children? At what point should an adult child assume total responsibility for his or her parents? When do adult children begin to manage the financial affairs of their elders in order to provide the best possible care, as well as to preserve the estate? Does a grandparent always have the right to give unsolicited advice about the raising of his grandchildren?

Maturity means, of course, being an adult. Physical maturity is in part the capacity to fulfill marital and parental responsibilities. It also implies a sense of self-worth. But not everyone achieves true maturity. Those who do know that it is constantly being tested by the vicissitudes of life—unhappy marriages, problem children, economic setbacks, failing health, widowhood. And not many of

101

us, at any age, can remain healthy, mature adults without the support of other people.

But it's very possible that our ideal concept of maturity is an unattainable dream—useful for controlling children, but of limited operational value throughout our lives. Most children, of any age, assume their parents will remain the adults forever, which makes it practically impossible to abdicate as a parent in old age, when we begin to need to be taken care of by those very children. Therefore, in a world like ours, where parents live to be so old, very often the assumption that the mother and father will always be the adults conflicts with reality. This holds particularly true when parents become infirm, incapable of caring for themselves, and, in many ways, somewhat childish.

But it's also true that many elderly people find it difficult to give up the assumption that simply because they are older than their offspring they will always be entitled to retain the parental, dominant role in the family. They feel they still have the right to tell their equally mature children what to do and how to do it. They are unable to accept the role reversals that of necessity take place when a parent becomes old.

With our increasing lifespans and higher incidence of divorce, the problem of who is to do the parenting in the family becomes so complex it is almost insoluble. And when a problem becomes complicated enough, people tend to avoid it, which only makes things worse.

SERMONETTE

Maturity and age are no longer necessarily related to each other. The increasing number of generations in any one family, the explosion of information systems, the changing child-rearing techniques, all make the generational progression too bumpy to keep the hierarchical system based solely on calendar years. In order to remain effective for all of its members, a family has to respect these changes by taking care of one another as the need arises, regardless of age or status. It is easier to allocate responsibilities in a family than to fragment it.

CHAPTER 24

EXCUSES, EXCUSES

"Oftentimes, excusing of a fault
doth make the fault the worse by the excuse."
Shakespeare, *King John* IV, ii

I have always felt that one of the joys of being a psychoanalyst was how much it taught us about ourselves and others. In our efforts to understand our own behavior, we began to understand other people better. Trying to "explain" became our favorite indoor sport. But, alas, we made the fatal mistake of using explanations as excuses. Indeed, I believe that much of the social chaos of the past forty years was caused by the prevalence of explanation and the absence of responsibility. We were so busy "understanding" our children that we made excuses for everything they did. We were too busy rationalizing their problems to impose any standards, any duties, any sense of what they owed the world. Fortunately for my own family, my wife believed in and followed the Ten Commandments—and insisted that her children live up to them.

To a great extent, society lost its old values and complicated explanations took the place of rightful indignation. But the problem was not limited to child rearing. Sexual infidelity was justified as a way of "working out a problem with the mother." New social judgments emerged. Almost every crime became "understandable."

104

Lovers were forgiven murdering one another because they felt "rejected." Harassment and aggression were seen as "acting out." Everybody talked interminably about childhood unhappiness, the inadequacy of parents, the cruelty of siblings, and sexual molestation by uncles, stepfathers, cousins.

But even if it were all true, and it usually was, "understanding" it precluded making any judgment or imposing any standards. And so life became that much more complicated and ambiguous. Furthermore, when our society decided that segments of the population deserved entitlements because of earlier discrimination, many people felt free to justify antisocial behavior by explaining it away as an example of social injustice.

As Judith Martin points out in her book *Common Courtesy*, "Curiously, it has never been harder to insult people intentionally. If you say, 'You are horrid and I hate you,' people reply, 'Oh, you're feeling hostile. I'll wait until you feel better.' Nonculpability, the idea that explaining motivation justifies any violation, is perhaps essential in a world of flying insults, where the all-purpose psychiatric excuse, 'I'm depressed,' is considered to absolve one of any obligation or responsibility."

Parents' responsibilities to their children, or adult children's responsibilities to their aging parents, are rationalized away whenever the perpetrators present excuses or explanations for their behavior. But their acts must be judged on their own merits.

Outside of the family, excuse-giving has also become a characteristic of American life: medical and psychiatric problems are used to excuse the breaking of leases, nonpayment of taxes, avoidance of jury duty, absence from work. Nobody is held responsible for anything, it seems. But a psychiatric explanation is no excuse for irresponsible behavior.

SERMONETTE

Life was simpler when people were judged by what they did, not by what led them to do it. The enormous value of insight is that it does help us to understand ourselves and to change—but it never justifies aberrant or unfair behavior. After all, we simply cannot live in one another's unconscious. The capacity to drop the excuses and learn to accept responsibility is essential in family unity.

CHAPTER 25

ON BEING UNIQUE, ON BEING IMMORTAL

*T*he denial of death plays a significant role in family life; nothing is more intrusive in the relations between parents and children than the expectation or possibility of the death of a parent. It conjures up many guilts, unconscious animosities, and deep feelings of loss. Even more disturbing to many of us, however, is the thought of our own death. Sigmund Freud pointed out that we all suffer from the delusion that death belongs to other people, not to us. He wrote that for strangers and enemies we do acknowledge death, and readily and unhesitatingly consign them to it. But, he added, the idea of our own passing is quite inaccessible to us. This fear of our own mortality creates in us the need to feel unique, for, if we're radically different from everyone else, we could somehow justify the belief that we are immortal.

How these illusions of uniqueness and immortality hamper family relationships! When members of the same family think they are different from the rest, it can create conflicts: comparisons, feelings of jealousy, resentment, and hostility.

One of the manifestations of this problem is the development in our minds of narcissistic fantasies about ourselves: we have a special insight into how the world works; we can see through people; we understand Reagan, or the current power figure, better than anybody else. Why do so many of us need to feel unique, heroic in dimension, to have the opportunity to be reborn in heaven, or to fantasize about a triumphant return to earth as a special spirit or as a hero? Is this a recent development? I would think not. It's been around for a long time; it's found in mythology and in the religions of the world, ancient and modern. Perhaps it's more intense now, since the "age of narcissism" of the 1920s and 1930s. But many decades before Freud had already documented the need of most children to deny their background and fantasize a background of royalty so they could feel unique and lovable. Children often deny the possibility of their parents' death because they cannot conceptualize survival without them. We have known for a long time that every infant needs to feel that his relationship to his mother is special.

Selma Fraiberg writes: "All love, even in later life, begins with exclusiveness. You are the only one that matters—only you." Most of us have this need to feel special, loved, cared for. The inability to accept mortality is related to this need to feel unique, to feel that we have nothing in common with anyone else, that our fate will be different from everybody else's.

My experience leads me to believe that the concept of immortality, or life after death, is meaningful to many people not as a religious concept, but as an opportunity for a reunion with lost loved ones. Most rational people nowadays tend to deny the persistence of this need to feel unique, but if their religion encourages it (by promising them that God will bless them particularly or that they will re-enter the world in a different, more special form), they will nevertheless unconsciously strive to become unique.

I relate these narcissistic, omnipotent fantasies to our attitudes toward death. Maybe "unique" is not the precise word, but I am constantly assaulted by the pervasive need of so many people to visualize themselves outside the framework of the ordinary or the banal. What most of us don't acknowledge are the problems these needs and subsequent fantasies can create in our lives. And the control we are able to exert over these powerful fantasies diminishes with age.

Our narcissistic illusions can poison the relationships, already full of competitive struggles, between fathers and sons. Fathers tend to deny their own mortality because of their narcissistic need to outsurvive their progeny as proof of their innate superiority.

In recent years, narcissism has played an increasingly prominent role in the diagnosis and treatment of many psychiatric disorders. Everywhere people are taken with their own inflated sense of self-importance. They have an insatiable need to be the center of attention. Many petty tyrants exist everywhere, and half the world is in a continual state of anger at their lack of recognition as unique by others. To them, death is the ultimate insult.

If civilized people have occasional glimpses into their inner grandiosity, they usually guard this secret against any possible exposure to the outside world. After all, it is rarely considered an acceptable posture among thoughtful people. One is expected to be modest, even while trying to write the great American novel or aspiring to be the sole political leader of the western world. But in family life, these restraints of modesty are totally abandoned.

In our individual inner worlds one doesn't necessarily have to feel superior in order to feel unique. In fact, the person may well believe that he is the worst, or even the most ordinary, of people—but this makes him special in some way. In his mind, he may have been the dumbest of all children, the most bashful, or the most vicious, or maybe he was the favorite child, or even the most rejected. The important thing is that he was in some way different and, therefore, special.

When an individual doesn't feel unique, he may compensate for his perceived deficiency by viewing himself as being favored by Lady Luck (if he is a gambler), or by using mood-altering drugs. Or he may find a feeling of uniqueness in religion. Most religions, except Buddhism and the old Hebraic religion, allow believers to project themselves into a world after death, and promise them untold pleasures and a special status for eternity. ''Immortality is the glorious discovery of Christianity,'' William Ellery Channing wrote in *Immortality*.

Interestingly, the most grandiose expectations are almost invariably found in the most humble patients, and more so as they grow older. Give me a patient who is depressed, unassuming, and who insists that he is only looking for some relief, and I am alerted to the underlying presence of the most unreasonable of fantasies. Scratch the surface of a defeated, pathetic, potentially suicidal patient and you will find he is making the most outlandish demands on life. When the possibility arises for some relief from his unfulfilled demands on life, it is never enough. Pursued to their logical conclusion, the expectations of such a man may be unlimited power, unlimited access to the most beautiful women (preferably in a harem), money beyond conception, and guarantees against any future illnesses or aging. And such a patient may appear before me humbly asking for "a little bit of happiness." The biggest frauds are always the most unassuming and humble.

But I am as deluded as my patients. It is hard for me to treat a patient unless I can convince myself that he has some special quality that seems worthy of exploring. It is hard to listen endlessly, to talk and explain *ad infinitum* without some rationale to justify all the effort (beyond income, which plateaus very early in a psychotherapist's practice). In a way, of course, it's true that we are all unique: there is only one of each of us in the world.

It is interesting to speculate on whether man's need to be the "chosen one," the favorite child, the wunderkind is not the basic cause of this phenomenon of the need to be immortal. No other species allows as long a period of dependency as we enjoy growing up. This does offer many special opportunities for the growth of human potential, but it also lays the groundwork for man's tragic fall. It seems that no girl ever feels loved enough while she is growing up, and no boy ever fails to feel insulted and humiliated in his early years.

People spend their whole lives fighting off death: jogging, dieting, going to church, finding the best doctors. I hear and read about people who are ready to die; I never meet them. The ones that I do meet don't really mean it. They hold on to some glimmer of hope, some form of restitution, some sudden cure, some transformation into another form, some expression of undying love.

And yet, on a rational level, people know that they are going to die and that they are not that special. But somehow they can't be totally realistic about the limits of their own biology. Woody Allen has said, "I'm not that afraid to die. I just don't want to be there when it happens." But people seem to have no problem at all accepting the mortality of others. Sigmund Freud liked to recall an anecdote in which a self-centered husband said to his wife: "If one of us dies, I shall move to Paris."

People usually die in the same way that they lived—in dignity or in chaos, in anger or in submission, in panic or in control. The end is a reflection of their life within the family. Perhaps one is less afraid to die if one was not afraid to live fully and to share of oneself with one's progeny. It would seem as if there is some correlation between the capacity to maintain good family relationships and the capacity to die peacefully.

Calmness about death may be life-saving. Highly dependent people lack the inner resources to sustain themselves, in life or in death. But facing our own mortality and taking good care of ourselves in a realistic manner can prolong our lives. For this, we need to let go of our fantasies of being unique and immortal; we need to accept the reality of death. Surrender to reality, or the refusal to surrender, actually has much more to do with attitudes toward living than toward dying. Indeed, being hard-nosed about death can bring about a positive, healthy, energized attitude toward life for the young or old, healthy or ill.

But since we cannot seem to conceptualize our own deaths, what are we to make of old age? After all, old age generally means that we're closer to death. But since nobody really knows how long life will be, of what use is this information? Usually, most people don't feel old until they retire, or until other people stop listening to them. As for infirmity, illness is incapacitating at any age and is no different when you're older. Indeed, many senior citizens are in better shape physically, financially, and intellectually than their middle-aged children.

People die at every age, and who is to say that the tragedies of the old are more poignant than the vicissitudes of the young? We should therefore try to enjoy the life we have left and share of ourselves with our families while we still can.

SERMONETTE

Most people really don't want to think about death. They frequently spend the better part of their lives trying to avoid thinking about the Grim Reaper. An acceptance of death is probably more painful if they have no family. So they try to feel that they are so unique that they will never die. And it's true that the most ordinary people carry the seeds of Ponce de Leon, Methuselah and Kotting Kohung.

If people try to feel unique because they cannot accept their biological limitations and need to turn to a deity to find salvation, so be it. But, as far as I am concerned, this is a failure to face life realistically and to fulfill our responsibilities to our families. It is a serious breach of our human commitments to one another as well as an unwillingness to accept the limitations of being human. Our commitments and responsibilities have to be primarily to one another, and if a person cannot confront his own biological limitations and has to create another persona or another world to give meaning to his life in this one, he will find it difficult to live a productive life and to leave the world a better place for his children.

CHAPTER 26

COURAGE

Mental illness is a failure of courage.

Alfred Adler

C owardice is one of the barriers that can prevent us from successfully adapting to family life. The absence of courage in intergenerational relationships can lead to misunderstandings and pain. But it's hard to be courageous; it's easier to give up one's identity and one's hopes in order to maintain peace within the family and to avoid conflict. How to compromise without giving in too much and becoming cowardly is one of the hardest tricks of being a good family member.

Fear of death, fear of losing contact with one's family, fear of being rejected, fear of growing poor, fear of becoming physically feeble—all of these may surface long before the events are even probable. Even before the anxiety becomes conscious, insecurity begins to be part of the posture of family life. Fears may then become self-fulfilling prophecies, clouding the family atmosphere.

Loss of courage is rarely discussed as such in the literature on psychotherapy; it is treated as a byproduct of other feelings, such as anxiety, depression, or obsession. But it might be valuable to examine courage as a separate emotion with its own distinctive qualities.

The inequality that exists between people is remarkable. In many ways, elderly people are even more disproportionate to one another than their younger counterparts. In clinical practice, we never stop wondering why one patient does so much better than another. Why does one child grow up "easier" than another? Why do some older people survive in their later years better than others?

There are many possible explanations for the disparity found in the levels functioning between people: sheer physical vitality, intelligence, the quality of parenting, the degree of insight, the nature of their education, their capacity to "fit in," the vicissitudes of chance, financial resources, the competence of their medical care, and, of course, the quality of their parents and the other role models about them. While these are all undoubtedly important factors, it seems to me that courage is another possible variable in the prognosis of effective functioning as we mature.

There is an enormous difference in the adventurousness and confidence of infants: about 15 percent of all newborns are timid, tense, avoid new challenges, and are afraid to be separated from their mothers. We begin to wonder if there isn't a genetic basis for the capacity to meet new challenges. If shyness is considered genetic by some researchers, there is no reason why courage might not be considered equally constitutional.

Courage is hard to define; its place in life is somewhat imprecise. It was first suggested to me as an explanation for failure by a rather imaginative patient, a struggling businessman in his mid-forties who suffered from a chronic mood disorder. When I first saw him in a depression and asked him what he thought was his most important problem, he responded, "I think I have a stomach disorder: I have no 'guts'." We both laughed. But getting to know this patient over a period of many years, he proved to me many times how right he was. Enormously well-liked, a clever raconteur, he was a bright and energetic man—but he truly did lack courage: when forced to deal with a business crisis, he always panicked; he could never confront his wife on a major issue; he raised his children by default; he managed to run his business by ingratiation, elaborate gift-giving, and constantly placating his employees. This patient never really made it in terms of financial success, though he managed to patch together a creditable life in his own charming way.

For years, like every therapist, I have been upset by the occasional patient who never quite manages to work out his problems even though all the ingredients seem to be at hand. Almost invariably, the timidity or failure of resolve of these patients goes back to the early relationship with their parents.

This may be an over-simplification, but I am now convinced that nobody succeeds, nobody gets better, nobody grows up, nobody lives graciously in their older years without some degree of courage. This is especially true as energy diminishes, aches and pains begin to appear, and our old props begin to disappear. In our younger years, it takes courage to leave home, to live alone, to try to make new friends, to open a business, to make a commitment, to jump off a diving board, to write a book, to make a sexual advance. But it takes even more courage to suffer physical infirmity, to grow old, to be widowed, or to live under economically diminished circumstances.

Unfortunately, it is hard to learn to be brave without experience; the older people who survive have usually taken risks, were adventurous, accepted responsibility when they were younger. The successful ones know their strengths, their limitations, and what to expect from the world about them. They have tested the waters in success and in defeat and are veterans of many minor wars.

The element of courage looms large in the relationship between parents and children. Without a good example of courage from their elders, how are the children supposed to learn to face their fears? And, in later years, many an older person finds restoration through the example set by his children.

Without this element of spirit, it is difficult to look anxiety in the face. One can have all the intellectual understanding in the world, but to confront your problems, to stare them down, to undo them, takes a lot of courage. I have watched endless numbers of people run away when confronted by their internal monsters. They could never get better unless they stopped being afraid of their own inner enemy. This is different from insight or even from the various forms of phobia. Sometimes it takes courage to turn on the light when you are frightened in a dark room. But without knowing the nature of our enemies or our fears, how can we face and defeat them?

Please do not misunderstand. I am not talking about aggressiveness, hostility, or being tough and loud. Anybody can learn those in two easy lessons, and they may or may not serve a useful purpose. I am talking about courage, and the fact that sometimes it takes more courage to keep quiet and do nothing than to act tough. The gutsiest experience of all is to resist temptation. Confucius said he hated people who thought themselves brave, when they were merely being unruly.

On a few rare occasions I have reached an impasse with a patient in which we were both at the end of our resources. He would look at me helplessly, as if to ask, ''Where do we go now, coach?'' Not infrequently, I have responded by telling him that the only thing left for him to do was to summon up enough courage from his inner self to go forward. I didn't know how he would do it, but, if he would try, I would spare no effort to help him. I have even told patients that I could not help them any further because they were too cowardly. Remarkable things happen when people hear such a remark about themselves.

In more playful moments in the office, patients have taunted me, accusing me of urging them to undertake tasks which were too frightening for them: ''It might be easy for you to do, it's impossible for me!'' I have then suggested that since they considered me so courageous, I would be glad to lend them some of my courage in order to get them started, but that they had to return the borrowings before the therapy was over. Some have.

Without insight and judgment, however, courage can be meaningless. You have to learn what is ''doable,'' and at the same time know what is impossible, impulsive, or self-destructive, because courage without judgment frequently leads to criminality.

SERMONETTE

Courage is a necessary element in family life. It provides leadership, and even solutions; when you reach an impasse, somebody's got to have the courage to find a new way of doing something, or of facing the realities of failure. When something's not right it takes courage for one family member to tell the other that it must be changed. But it's hard to learn about courage on one's own. We all borrow new techniques of adaptation through contact with people who are willing to lend their wisdom and experience to the potential sufferer. The maintenance of lines of communication with others is the best possible guide.

Too often, older people are expected to be cowardly, and respond accordingly. Just as a good parent teaches a child to be courageous, so an adult child, like a good psychiatrist, can lend his courage to a frightened older person. They can offer an umbrella, a role model under which courage can be developed with protection and guidance. In this way, the early failures of the elderly can be diffused until the fledgling older pupil learns to develop the courage necessary to face the challenges of life. Maybe they will have to be alone for a while, maybe they will have to learn new tricks, maybe they will need emotional or physical care. But, with help, they can do it.

We live in a frightening world. We each have our own choices and our own compass to follow, often alone. But there are no rewards for not trying. And, in the end, we find that taking chances and courageously facing our fears was not so frightening after all.

In *Of Death*, Francis Bacon wrote: "He that dies in an earnest pursuit is like one that is wounded in hot blood, who, for the time, scarce feels the hurt; and therefore a mind fixed and bent upon somewhat that is good doth avert the dolors of death."

CHAPTER *27*

GOLF AND THE SEXUAL REVOLUTION

*G*olf is an interesting sport, especially for mature people. It is possible to play it without unusual physical endurance, and it is a good excuse for a walk in the country. One of the few sports which allows families to play together, it does not depend upon physical strength or natural grace, both of which have practically nothing to do with golfing skill. And, in the process, it allows for some social interaction with a selected group of friends, usually from very similar backgrounds to one's own. The challenge of trying to land the golf ball in that small hole using a variety of misshapen clubs and employing those unnatural swings, so laboriously learned—all of this makes golf endearing to otherwise proper citizens. And golf satisfactorily performs the basic function of most weekend games: to diffuse the tensions of daily life through frivolous activity.

But golf and country clubs also reveal interesting aspects of family life. Their impact on the relations between the generations is quite apparent, and everybody agrees that adult children seem to be loath to participate in country club activities with their parents. The reasons would seem to be obvious—they presumably cannot stand the elitism, the snobbishness, the exclusivity of that lifestyle. But these reasons fail to explain why children will join other clubs of equal snobbishness on their own, or why they will go with their

118

parents on expensive cruises, or why they will gladly sail with their parents on a yacht. It's really not the snobbishness which turns them off; it's the youthful, or even adolescent, behavior of their parents at the golf club which gets to them. The activities at a country club encourage gaiety, conviviality, silly outfits, much dancing, and excessive drinking. "Why does my mother talk about the 'girls' when she's on the phone with somebody from the country club?" a bewildered adult child might ask. "They're dignified old ladies, but act so childish when they talk about golf!"

Life at the golf club has connotations associated with the embarrassment of early sexuality—laughing, flirtatiousness, playfulness—which the younger generation cannot tolerate to witness in their elders. Most people today can accept the sexuality of older people, but it's a rare child who can tolerate witnessing his parents in a publicly flirtatious situation. It's as if each generation were embarrassed to accept the sexuality of the one before or after.

There is another aspect of family life that manifests itself in the game of golf and which is worthy of comment: one spouse's concern over the other's physical decline. As an aging male golfer, I would like to give my impressions.

A favorite sport of older men (especially those who are retiring to the South), golf usually ends up as the ultimate insult for the physically failing male: what is worse than to build your retirement plans about an athletic pursuit which is doomed from the start? For no sooner does the retiring man dedicate himself to improving his game than his physical infirmities begin to reveal themselves. I can read books for as long as I live without embarrassment; nobody knows whether I can see or understand what I am reading. But golf is a public display of one's prowess or weakness—there is no place to hide in this game.

Until I was widowed, I always played with "the men." I had no objection to playing with "the girls," but my wife was always too sensible to want to play golf. In the early years, she made an abortive attempt, but she never really wanted to play and was finally banished from the course for picking flowers while on a round of golf. It seemed to me like an act of disloyalty to be playing with other women, and I guess nobody really asked me. I think they were intimidated by my wife.

I recollect now how easy it was to avoid personal contact with other women while I was married. I rarely danced with other women, and nobody really complained about my apparent shyness at parties. They assumed that either I was an extremely devoted husband or that my wife was insanely jealous. I have no such choices now; I am expected to be "civilized," that is, to interact with others and to be gracious.

I have tried to accept my new station in life by occasionally playing golf in friendly, mixed groups. This usually includes a married couple, a single older woman (almost invariably a widow), and myself. This is known as a "mixed foursome." It is amazing how four older people can have such a good time together in an athletic event in spite of their age.

It's really quite interesting to play golf under my new condition as bachelor, especially in a game where none of us is really competent. We all play fairly inconsistently, our scores are excessive, but we all take it terribly seriously. The golf course is beautiful, the married couples all seem very dedicated to one another, and everyone involved seems content to be spending time together. We are enjoying a day in the outdoors, convinced that we are doing something very healthy. And older men and women enjoy one another's company in a traditional sport like golf because it is well within the parameters of their physical capacity and cushions them from their differences thanks to a computerized handicap system which allows one to play against one's established game, not against a competitor's.

No other sport would seem to be less sexist, and yet I have become increasingly aware of the interesting phenomena that occur when men and women play golf together. It comes out most dramatically when one of us hits a bad shot, especially off the tee. When men play alone nobody seems to care when one misses a shot (excluding tournaments, of course). One of the players may make some standard remark, but nobody really cares. Nothing is really at stake.

The other men may mumble a reassurance, or a casual insult, but they are really more preoccupied with their own game. Or, at worst, the duffer will lose some meaningless amount of money to his competitor.

But when men play with women, the emotional response to a bad shot escalates dramatically, depending on which gender has made the mistake. It's as if we were playing in a different emotional arena. A whole new set of parameters comes into play: men seem less patient with themselves when they goof, and reassurances from their male partners are less forthcoming; women seem upset when their husbands lose their golfing form, rattled when they spoil a shot. In fact, when I play better than my opposing male in a mixed foursome, it seems to me that the wife frequently seems annoyed with her husband; she seems more upset by his inadequacy than he is. The husband somehow never seemed as upset when he was playing alone with the men.

Almost invariably in mixed games, the men players are unnecessarily protective of the women, spending an inordinate amount of time explaining and apologizing for the bad shots of the women. They are continually reassuring them, although many women are actually better golfers than men. Still, women are constantly being told, ''Take a Mulligan,'' or ''You were distracted, try again.''

I think that this behavior on the golf course is related to how the sexes react to the aging process in their spouses. Somehow, on the golf course we witness how difficult it is for most older women to tolerate the increasing physical failings of their husbands. All of the older women have many widowed friends, and the prospect of that happening to them is never acceptable. Even worse, many married women spend their later years nurturing a physically ailing husband, and somehow the bad golf shot raises the awful specter of male failure and dependency.

Why do the physical failings of the wives seem less threatening than those of the men? It's almost as if diminishing power in older women is more acceptable than it is in men. In any event, it seems to momentarily reestablish the traditional male image, and the unexpressed attitude of the men is, ''What can we do to help? Please don't be upset!''

It's really very hard to break old habits, and even harder to give up myths of male superiority. And it's hard for women to give up the need to play Cinderella. We still try to protect women when they are already quite superior to us in so many ways. In our marriages, we still try to protect our wives from their failures. The sexual revolution waxes and wanes, women gradually become surer of themselves, but we still cannot accept the changing hierarchical structure within marriage. Men encourage the traditional posture, especially when they are more financially successful; and most golf clubs are still very male-oriented. As women develop their own strengths, it becomes more and more difficult, with increasing age, to maintain the old balance (or is it imbalance?) of power. I am hard put to think of many older couples where the woman isn't having trouble maintaining an attitude of respect for her husband's so-called superiority. But most of the people I know have good manners, and naked disrespect is fortunately rarely seen, particularly on the golf course. It's always surprising to me to find how much such a simple game can tell us about family life and male-female interactions.

SERMONETTE

We pay a high price for the presumed superiority of men. Maybe it's time to give it up. Maybe it's time to change the handicapping system.

CHAPTER 28

THE REBIRTH OF MONOGAMY

"Happy families are all alike; every unhappy family is unhappy in its own way." Count Leo Tolstoy, *Anna Karenina*

I would like to discuss happy marriages and what makes them so alike, so similar that they may even seem boring. Perhaps if we can understand how they manage to survive we can learn how to make our own relationships better.

The recent appearance of AIDS and its epidemic spread has brought pause to the sexual revolution. Among the two million Americans who may die this year, AIDS will claim more than its share, and we are now more afraid of AIDS than of any other cause of death. Casual sex is rapidly becoming a less reputable way of life. Monogamy (heterosexual or homosexual) is on the verge of coming back into fashion: people have gone back to marrying at an earlier age; couples try harder to stay together; singles are becoming suspect. The fear of contagion may do what the fear of God could not: bind couples together till death do them part.

There are many problems with this return to monogamy and fidelity, however. For instance, how many members of the younger adult generation really know what monogamy is all about? It has been out of fashion for too long, and many of their parents were divorced during the sexual revolution. In any event, they have relatively few role models available to emulate. They may not even be sure if monogamy ever really existed; and if it did, how did those archaic people manage to make it work?

Some of my patients, as well as my friends, claim they've never known a happily married couple, and they don't really believe the old black-and-white movies on late-night TV. They believe that Hollywood contrived the whole mythology as an escape from the Depression of the 1930s and that the romantic novels of the nineteenth century always went from romance to tragedy.

Having known both of these periods, I would like to presume to describe my clinical impressions. Having lived through the Depression, the rise and fall of Greta Garbo, the sexual revolution, the Woodstock rebellion, and President Reagan, I feel it is my entitlement.

It is difficult to define how anything works: it's much easier to discover faults, imperfections, or disease—and it seems to be so much more fun as well. The positive ingredients of anything that works, including a good marriage, sound so mushy, nice, platitudinous. It's a bit like trying to describe good health, or the perfect Boy Scout. I don't know that I have all the answers; defining the elements of a good relationship is a big bite to chew.

Before I begin, one statement in self-defense: In 1953, I was the first author to challenge the standards of the marriage manuals of the time with my book, *Paradoxes of Everyday Life*. I knew that I was happily married, yet I'd never meet the standards of T. H. Van der Velde, author of the popular manual, *The Ideal Marriage*. Up until then, everybody was afraid to admit that the "normal" standards were impossible to attain. Since I was the first one to stand up and be counted as a failure by the standards of Havelock Ellis, I feel that I have a license to talk about the parameters of the attainable.

There seem to be certain basic ingredients which most of the old-fashioned successful marriages had in common. What are they?

Let us test Tolstoy's thesis that all families are alike in their happiness and in their unhappiness:

The partners enhanced each other's lives. A marriage has a better chance of success if each partner brings something different (perhaps unique, or special) to the union that the mate cannot attain alone. It may be intellectual, social, sexual, or financial. Two people find it easier to stay together when the quality of their life together exceeds the value of the sum of the parts. It represents the ticket of admission to the show; nothing is for free, they each have to contribute something to the entertainment.

This proposition works even in the new equality. It seemed less true in the old days, when so frequently one partner completely dominated and the lesser one played a more servile sexual or housekeeping role. But we must remember that even playing an inferior, masochistic role is a contribution to the meaning of the life of a sadist. If each spouse enhances the other's lifestyle far beyond what either could accomplish by himself, the relationship already contains at least one essential ingredient for success.

Marriage is the ultimate *quid pro quo*. If the combination of the two people doesn't allow for an interchange of some kind, there is no real point in those two people being together. This presumes that both members not only have something to give, but also know how to take.

Presumably, then, if two people are identical, they bring nothing special to each other and therefore have no marriage. Sexual differences, anatomical or physiological, intellectual differences, varieties of emotional expression, these are all spices that add to the possibility of a happy marriage. Whether it be in a successful heterosexual or homosexual marriage, each partner brings some different attitude, style, or intellect which enhances the lifestyle of the other. I wonder if older people don't become bored with each other because the years flatten out their differences.

It's hard to say what any two people are doing for each other; it's a unique balance for each couple. The needs of people are very complicated and byzantine and no simplistic generalizations are universally applicable. But without these reciprocities, there is no real marriage.

They gave each other pleasure, sexually and otherwise. No good marriage survives unless the partners give each other significant pleasure. Beyond producing orgasms and having children, the sexual life is very complicated in marriage and takes many forms, all of which are important to its survival.

Leaving out the phenomenon of direct sexual contact, how can one describe the qualities of experience of two people who just enjoy being in each other's presence? It is one of the most significant elements of two people living together. But whatever it is, no couple can survive if they don't enjoy being close to each other. Under normal circumstances, the enjoyment of each other's presence leads to their sexual arousal and interest in each other. In recent decades, people have tried to reverse the sequence; they have tried to become intimate with companions with whom they have already had sex. This is much less likely to lead to a successful relationship.

There are three kinds of sex in the lifetime of a marriage: a) Romantic love, with sex. Everybody agrees that these feelings have a short lifespan within a marriage, perhaps a few years. They are spontaneous, emotional, and explosive, and are dangerous only if either partner expects them to last forever or to solve all of the problems that may arise within the relationship. b) Lust. These feelings may last for an extended period, even in relationships between people who claim that they are no longer in love. If combined with a commitment to each other, a good sexual match is an adequate substitute for romantic love. It then becomes only a semantic problem. c) Tenderness, intimacy, affection. I'm not sure if these feelings should be included as sexual, because they certainly exist in nonsexual relationships. In an ongoing relationship, they serve as an alternative to genital sex. The traditional man avoided any such displays except as a preliminary for sexual intercourse because he didn't believe that he should start anything he couldn't finish, and he expected that sex without orgasm was effeminate. The traditional woman would frequently become promiscuous because of her need for affectionate contact. She was not permitted to be a "tease" or flirtatious without being expected to have full sexual relationships. Many old-fashioned women would be willing to "pay the price" out of their need to be close to somebody. The ability to separate tenderness from sex is a distinctive quality of a good marriage.

How to combine these three diverse sexual elements is the miracle of a good relationship. How to fold one phase into the next without disruption and without constantly seeking new partners is the ultimate form of maturity. If one canot have both sacred and profane love within the same relationship then multiple relationships become the only alternative.

Two people giving each other pleasure cannot be equals at all times. Sometimes the passions may be uneven, and, temporarily, one or the other may only be behaving generously when responding to the other's request for sex.

When monogamy continues into the later years, or even begins then, special factors come into operation in the sexual life. All kinds of new combinations become possible: romance without orgasm, tenderness without passion, women having orgasm without the men sharing. Many variations are possible; each is valid if it serves to enhance the lives of the people involved.

They learned how to fight constructively. The capacity to keep the emotional and intellectual juices flowing in a marriage is directly related to the capacity to disagree and fight without destroying each other. Nothing keeps the excitement alive, nothing serves as an antidote to boredom more than a good difference of opinion—except, of course, when the fighting becomes serious.

An illustration: the man sounds frantic on the telephone. He must see me immediately, his world is collapsing. When he finally appears, he is shaken, his hands are tremulous, he has a two days' growth of beard and he is obviously suffering from a hangover. "My wife walked out on me two days ago," he tells me. "We were so happy together, married for four years. Now I don't know where she is, can't find her. One argument, and she said that she couldn't stand it any more. One fight and it was all over. Oh, I know I was no angel. Please, please, try to help me. I need her back."

I have been a witness to a variation of this tragic scene at least a half dozen times. It's always the same story. Occasionally I am fortunate enough to persuade the wife to come in to see me. When she finally appears in the office, she usually presents a horrendous story of an unhappy marriage filled with a variety of cruelties on the part of her husband ranging from gambling, drinking, and chasing other women to stinginess and assorted minor cruelties. When she finishes her laundry list of abuses and I turn to her husband, he usually eagerly admits the truth of most of the accusations. "But we were so happy. Why didn't she tell me she was so miserable? I would have tried to do something about it."

"He should have known what he was doing to me," she retorts. "I never wanted a marriage where I was fighting all the way. My whole childhood was filled with the bickering of my parents. I was trying to have a peaceful and loving marriage. He was impossible."

We have now described the one-fight marriage, where the first fight is the last fight. It is the killer. Fortunately, most marriages survive the first fight. A few are even peaceful. But most successful marriages survive because the couple has learned to fight successfully. I will try to define the parameters of constructive fighting within our ever-imperfect relationships and marriages.

I believe that marriages stand or fall on how they handle negative feelings. Anger is the key emotion, and husbands and wives handle it differently. But the handling of other negative emotions—fear, hate, disgust, sadness—is also crucial. Women are found to be much more direct and confrontational; men try to deflect negative feelings, and cope with them less effectively. Women nag, men sulk. Escalation and de-escalation seem also to be crucial. I read in a *New York Times* article on this topic that couples who are happy possess the ability to de-escalate conflict. Importantly, men seem to suffer more physically from the impact of the stress of confrontation than do women.

In order to understand why women are more capable of withstanding confrontation than men one has to understand the many meanings of words. Words are like bullets. They can kill. And they can never be called back. Words seem to have greater lethal power when women use them against men, perhaps because men speak later and are less articulate. Women, who tend to use language more freely, seem to have a greater resistance to the sharp edges of words. Whatever the reason, women seem more able to deal with words, positive or negative, with greater facility.

But regardless of who gets hurt more, it is obvious that some marriages are not capable of surviving the occasional angry interchange that is necessary for the continuation of any decent relationship. It's all very well to talk about humor or a good sex life as a compensation, but there is no avoiding the fact that learning how to fight is one of the most basic ingredients of any good marriage.

Keeping the fight small and learning to de-escalate are useful, but they beg the basic issue. The one central element of survival is "Avoid the jugular!" Every married couple knows the killing spot, the Achilles Heel, of the spouse. One can fight and argue forever as long as one avoids the fatal shot which mortally wounds the opponent. Fighting can be fun, sexually exciting; it can even resolve many problems. The trick is to avoid the one fatal argument which blows up the marriage forever. Different people can be criticized in different ways, but marriage partners should carefully avoid the other's weak spot. I know mine very well; my wife never touched it. I knew hers; I never touched it. Thus, we fought endlessly and harmlessly, always avoiding the fatal blow, but resolving all the other problems. Maybe one of the true tests of love is knowing the weak spot of the other and always avoiding it.

The mouth, while it can kill, is also the catalyst for many of the special things that happen between people. Great thoughts and tender feelings emit from it. It is, however, hard to learn how to use words as conduits for affection and tenderness; it is easier to yell and scream. But no relationship ever matures without learning how to disagree. Honest contention without mortal wounding is one of the great aphrodisiacs. Unexpressed rage is a great sexual turnoff.

There is no question that nobody knows their partner until they have had their first fight. More things come out during a good fight than during any other single human interaction. People who are in love should defer any commitments until they have had their first big argument. Until then, they are still strangers. For there is no human love without ambivalence.

A married couple that has learned to deal with the differences and hostilities between them has set an example for their children which will allow future generations to survive with one another on a functioning level.

They stayed awake, kept each other's minds alive. The ultimate aphrodisiac is the human mind. Its use is the most effective way of maintaining any relationship. Hormones can fluctuate, breasts can sag, income can be unpredictable, children can bring pride or shame, but ultimately the married couple must deal with each other. Without some intellectual exchange it is hard to keep the marriage alive.

To accomplish this, it becomes necessary for the couple to communicate. In sharing thoughts and feelings, at least one of the two partners has to listen and at least one has to talk, preferably alternately. Too many people in relationships presume that the other is a mind reader. The lack of awareness of each other's consuming ideas and passions is frequently the cause of very stubborn problems. It is a source of constant amazement to me that people can live together for years and still not be able to read each other, but then I remind myself that they never did talk.

Passionate joint activities may serve as a substitute for communication. But if this is limited to a mutual interest in the welfare of the children, it is usually effective for only a limited period of time; certainly not after the children leave the home. We have all seen the silent couples in the best restaurants, on the expensive cruises, quietly enjoying themselves without communicating with each other. The impression remains that people who don't talk to each other sleep quietly in separate beds. We must learn how to communicate, stimulate our partner intellectually, if we are to remain interested in each other and if the union is to survive.

They were on each other's side. The feeling that one's mate is on one's side—that each is concerned with the other's welfare—sounds very simple, and it is. Except that people also have to be loyal to themselves sometimes, as well as to old friends, and, most difficult of all, to their blood relatives—the children and parents competing for their loyalty. This question becomes more complicated as marriages become circuitous; more so with the endless combinations of new and old marriages, of parenthood within serial marriages, of new and old children. It is a complex tapestry, yet the people who remain happily married manage to balance the competing forces of loyalty versus disloyalty. In the end, there has to be no question of the loyalty of one mate to the other if the relationship is to survive.

I am reminded of a major argument in the marriage of one of my patients. The couple was suffering as a result of their teenaged children's delinquencies. The couple was in bed arguing in the dark over the question of how to discipline one of the children for an infraction of house rules. It was an issue only because the man tended to be more lenient than his wife; it was probably one of the few issues over which they ever really fought. The wife was more traditional, while my patient was trying to be a rational, twentieth-century father. On this particular evening, the disagreement became a threatening thing, and the father found himself blurting out that they were skating on thin ice. He argued that they were both related to their children by blood, genes, and love, and could not escape or deny their responsibility to them. On the other hand, their relationship with each other was only a legal arrangement and potentially fragile. The two of them were strangers who met in adult life and fell in love, but were only bonded by a piece of paper: a marriage license. Too many people at that time were dissolving this bond with the greatest of ease.

Since they were irrevocably stuck with the children for life, there was no point in challenging their own, much more fragile, marital relationship by disagreeing over them. They each compromised, deciding to be good to themselves and their marriage. In so doing, they undoubtedly helped their children, for nothing upsets the progeny more than the awareness that the parents' marriage is at their mercy.

They made a conscious effort to make their union work. After years of trying to reconcile unhappy marriages, I am convinced that there is no such thing as emotional incompatibility. If two people decide that they want to make their marriage work, they can almost always succeed despite outrageous differences. It is usually a conscious, voluntary decision; every spouse knows what he can do to please or displease the other. If they decide to stop trying, and break up their relationship, usually nothing can be done. If the wife decides that she doesn't want a poor or impotent husband, if the man decides he doesn't want to live with a grouchy wife, no amount of therapy can be helpful. If one or both partners choose to be impossible, they usually know what they are doing. It is fruitless to try to reconcile a marriage where one partner is disinterested; if they want to preserve their marriage, they usually know what to do—or what not to do. Nobody has to tell them to send flowers on their wedding anniversary or to give up their extramarital relationship.

For many years, I have refused to undertake treatment of any patient with marital problems unless the partner will also commit to the preservation of the marriage and make himself available for consultation. I have been burnt too often to allow a patient to struggle endlessly and for naught when the opposing spouse has no intention of helping to accomplish a reconciliation.

No relationship is ever set for life; it has to be nurtured by constant effort toward renewal. No relationship to spouse, children, or friends can ever be taken for granted, and the longer you know a person who is important to you, the harder it is to keep renewing it. It's very easy to impress somebody when you first meet them, but it's different with a partner you've known for decades, or with a child who has heard every corny joke in your armamentarium.

They respected each other. Women used to have to respect their husbands, or pretend that they did, in order to maintain the stability of the traditional marriage; this was less true for the men. Today, very few marriages survive where the woman doesn't admire, respect, or even adore her husband. But now most men also want to feel the same way about their wives. Men used to need respect, and they still do; now women want it too.

For most women, the loss of respect for their mate is a turnoff. This problem becomes especially difficult in the older years, when the men stop working, their sexual powers diminish faster, and they become ill, often fatally, while their wives are still vigorous.

With men it seems to be different; the man's capacity to live happily with a woman is not directly related to his respect for her. But with the liberation of women, more men admire their wive's talents and seem to be more capable of accepting their weaknesses (in fact, some prefer them). I think it's time for everybody to start sincerely respecting one another.

They used the same compass. There is one aspect of a happy marriage which I have been unable to define until only recently. It would never have occurred to me if I hadn't been widowed.

Several years ago, I had finished a manuscript and was quite excited, even elated. But when I reached for the phone I suddenly found that I had nobody to call. There were plenty of people around—I have children, grandchildren, friends, colleagues, a literary agent—but nobody would have really shared my excitement with me in the way my wife would. When I had this closeness with another person, I never thought about it, I presumed that it was part of normal life. Apparently, it's not.

I realized that my wife and I had been using each other for years as sounding boards, as sharers of dreams, as navigational points of reference, that our lives revolved about each other in a way that could only be compared to having a mutual, built-in compass. It had nothing to do with honesty, sharing, kindness, or love. We were simply in tune with each other as a point of reference, the way a navigator fixes his course by finding the North Star. It had nothing to do with truth or caring; it had to do with sharing life with only one person at a time. A shifting compass is vertiginous.

Spheres of influence, or the politics of marriage. One of the problems of equality, whether it be in marriage or in any other area, is that nobody can ever be totally on a par with his partner. At the same time, it is also true that each person may have special attributes which differentiate him or her from the rest.

Most enlightened people in modern relationships seem to be striving to find some degree of reasonable accommodation, difficult though this may be. Some men take pleasure in trying to care for the children, working in the kitchen, or shopping for groceries. Women no longer avoid balancing the checkbook, being active in politics, or repairing the kitchen sink. As people grow older, it is harder to maintain the traditional differences between the sexes.

But the achievement of total equality is really quite impossible. Most people tend to be equal in their diversity, multiplicity, and scattering of talents. If two equals could be found, could they ever get along? Equality is not only hard to achieve, it tends to be a fiercely competitive thing, or even worse, it can become quite boring. There are no true equals; we can only help one another to compensate for deficiencies. In any equitable marriage, one partner has to be prepared to lend a helping hand to the other.

The true test of democracy is its capacity to survive diversity of talent, anatomy, and intellect. Any attempt to equalize everything is an exercise in futility. *Vive la différence.*

In the absence of a comfortable diversity, a balance of power becomes the only alternative. We have learned, only too sadly, that nobody is to be trusted with ultimate authority; it is always abused. Authoritarianism has to be replaced by "spheres of influence," as Count Metternich might have suggested; otherwise, nothing will ever get done. Equality is just too difficult to maintain, and the endless search for it leads to constant conflict.

The real problem is usually the prejudices which we have built into our conceptions of masculinity and femininity. The capacity to step out of the stereotypes is the only alternative. Who carries out the garbage, who drives the car more skillfully, who makes more money, all of these are problems that people of good will can manage to solve. But there are two problem areas which seem more difficult than most.

One of these areas is the raising of children. Children seem to need, or at least prefer, two parents who are not carbon copies of each other. Somehow the myth has developed that children are deeply disturbed by their parents' disagreements. But what better way is there for children to prepare to meet the world than learning how to play one parent against the other? That's what life is all about. There is nothing more oppressive to a growing child than to face two united, determined parents who are playing at being democratic.

The other problem brought up by democracy and equality is that commonality can be so boring. Many people love doing things by themselves sometimes; in fact, most creative activities demand privacy. Many a marriage has deteriorated for want of privacy, or "space." If this is interpreted as rejection by one's partner, the couple is in trouble.

The creative use of diversity helps to achieve a balance of power. Moments of equality—playing tennis together, putting together a collection—then become the exception which proves the rule. To quote Machiavelli, "Republics have a longer life and enjoy better fortune than principalities because they can profit by their greater internal diversity. They are better able to meet emergencies."

SERMONETTE

That's how it used to be in the old days of monogamy. The above are the elements of successful marriages that I was able to identify. But do we honestly believe that it is possible to return to such an age of innocence? If we are to avoid the AIDS epidemic, we may have no choice.

If monogamy is inevitable, we have to try to make it work. It really isn't such a painful process. Other methods have failed to make us happy: promiscuity hasn't worked, serial marriages are exceedingly complicated, and romanticism is too simplistic and never lasts (the romance tales of the past ended with "And they lived happily ever after," but nobody ever told us how to accomplish this!).

It would be nice if every marriage was always forever, but obviously this is no longer possible. Only the possibility of divorce keeps some marriages viable. If a marriage is in danger, every attempt should be made to renew the couple's dedication to each other. Without this dedication, we are back to loneliness and sickness.

It's nice to know that it's possible for two people to live their adult lives together. But it would seem that we are now trying to build families without real commitment. This is really too difficult. I think that the old way is still possible—if we are to preserve monogamy. As in mothering, new forms of marriage are appearing, homosexual as well as heterosxual. The same principles apply to all.

CHAPTER 29

WHAT ABOUT SIGMUND FREUD?

*M*any people believe that psychoanalysis has become obsolete. They compare it to the Spanish Empire in the sixteenth century, which lost control of the new world because of its stultifying orthodoxy and inquisitorial preoccupation with heresy. The new competitors of psychoanalysis—psychoactive drugs, cognitive-behavioral therapy, family therapy, and a variety of other approaches—have carved out their competing empires in the brave new world of psychotherapy.

The decline of the theories of Sigmund Freud also seems to parallel the general loss of respect for patriarchy, even as the decline of Molly Goldberg signaled the increasing disinterest in traditional mothering. We may disagree with some of Freud's ideas, or the value of insight, but the human qualities which he brought to his profession—he was a concerned parent, a non-punitive person, a man who tried to understand what went wrong with patients and family, an advocate of the patient—represented an era which somehow we have lost through the decline of the importance of the father figure.

There is today a great amount of criticism of Freud's theories, but people tend to forget that probably the best thing he accomplished was to bring an image of concern—of paternity—to every problem he faced. His followers tended to exaggerate his theoretical ideas and to neglect the very benign, humane, masculine qualities which were his ultimate therapeutic tool. Some of these qualities, taken out of the theoretical context, are the things that we miss in our fathers today. It is unfortunate that Freud was never willing to accept the human need to rely on one another and tended to categorize all dependency needs, such as religion, as essentially neurotic.

Sigmund Freud was very important to my generation independent of any of his theoretical formulations. In addition to the deep social changes brought about by the youth and women's movements of the 1960s, the decline of Freud's ideas was inevitable in the light of the new technological developments in neurobiology, which he himself predicted would some day replace psychoanalysis. Yet the practice of psychiatry, and, more specifically, of psychotherapy and psychoanalysis, flourishes even as neuro-biological-chemical research extends our understanding and treatment of mental illness. More and more people today seem to be reaching for some kind of person-to-person therapy, usually a psychotherapeutic method derived from traditional psychoanalysis. What's more, the same type of talking therapy first developed by Sigmund Freud seems to continue to develop in one variation or another in ever-widening circles.

This paradox of apparent obsolescence and simultaneous rebirth and expansion into new forms leads us to the question of what exactly is the relevance of Freud's theories to the family today. Maybe the answer can tell us something about how we really feel about ourselves and our families, and why Sigmund Freud was once so important to so many of us.

There has never been any question about the widespread need for personal help, but the theories of psychoanalysis and psychotherapy, their effectiveness, and their costs have been under continual attack, and their scientific basis is questioned at least once a week in the *New York Times*. The integrity of its practitioners is constantly under scrutiny. And yet comparative studies indicate that all forms of psychotherapy seem to work in their own way, especially when the practitioner is dedicated to his work and the patient is hopeful of improvement. The range of applicability of any one method is open to question. The current direction being taken by psychotherapy is away from individual therapy and increasingly inward in the direction of genetics and neurobiology—and outward toward sociological issues. The world is less interested in the unique psychological qualities of each individual and the vicissitudes of his personal development. The psychotherapies are accused of being too expensive, and the government and the insurance companies are trying to distance themselves from the costs of their applications.

Despite all of these doubts and moral questions, I have been practicing this discipline—psychodynamic psychotherapy—for over forty-five years, and would like to make a few personal anecdotal comments. I presume that the fact that I have been in practice for so long gives my opinions no great authenticity—because I could be as self-deluded and self-serving as anybody else. But I am convinced that Freud started a dynamic process which we still emulate for good reason, whether we are aware of it or not.

The concept of psychoanalysis was developed in Vienna during the last decade of the nineteenth century, almost single-handedly by Sigmund Freud. He psychoanalyzed my analyst, Abram Kardiner, in the 1920s, so I consider him my scientific grandfather. He was the first healer of mental illness (medical or otherwise), and was a clever and courageous man, establishing a body of knowledge that formed the foundation of the first of the modern psychotherapies. Freud's influence is so profound in our lives and culture that it is hard to conceive of the hiatuses which existed before his time. Along with Marx and Darwin, he was one of the great intellectual movers of the nineteenth century.

Many of Freud's ideas have been challenged. He made some mistakes, did some foolish things (as every biographer is quick to rediscover and document). But despite flaws in theory, and even in personality, he left behind a significant heritage, much of which is indestructible. The following are some highly personal comments on what I consider some of the permanent contributions of Sigmund Freud, and how we can benefit from them in our daily lives:

Freud listened to the patient. Nobody before him had ever tried to listen in a systematic way to what the patient had to say, trying to not inject his own personal views. Before him, nobody had ever really bothered to listen to the patient at all: doctors preached to their patients, bled them, shouted at them—but never listened. And Freud also taught himself to listen with intelligence. Most people are too busy talking, or preparing a speech or a response in their minds, to concentrate on what the other person is saying. He offered his patients an interested audience—a rare event in the life of anybody, neurotic or otherwise.

We, too, can learn how to listen, without expectations, judgments, or preconceptions, to what our family members and friends are trying to say to us. If we make the effort to listen objectively, intelligently, respecting the other person's desires and feelings—whether we agree with them or not—we can find a way to work out our problems together, instead of imposing our wishes on everyone around us.

He continued to listen. Freud seemed to have endless time and patience. He never expected to solve problems overnight, and dedicated himself to the long-range perspective. He did not believe in quick fixes or magic solutions.

In the same way, when dealing with any sort of conflict within the family, we must realize that deep and lasting change cannot take place overnight. We must exercise patience with both ourselves and others when the messages aren't coming across clearly at first.

(An aside: Listening is not an easy thing, even for trained therapists; it is a skill we must all work to acquire. One of the most frequent complaints from my patients has been: "Why do I have to pay you for listening to me? Couldn't any good friend so the same for me?" I usually agree with the patient, just to be difficult. But I challenge him to find a friend who will listen to him for three hours a week for an indefinite future. If this doesn't faze him, I then challenge him to find a friend who will not get angry when he does not follow the advice given. If he is not flabbergasted yet, I then suggest that he find a friend who will not sooner or later use the confidential information for some kind of personal advantage or one-upmanship. I then suggest that maybe he could find a priest or a rabbi who would have time to listen to him for more than twenty minutes. And finally, I present him with a quote from one of my favorite patients, who suffered from recurrent depressions: "A friend in need is a pain in the ass!")

Freud tried to interpret what his patients were saying. Once he thought he understood what he had heard, Freud tried to transmit it back to the patient in the form of an interpretation. He digested what he heard, filtered it through his own ample intelligence, and returned it to the patient in a coherent explanation. There are some who believe that being understood by the therapist is probably more important to the patient than understanding himself—finally, somebody knows what they are trying to say!

When we try to communicate with one another, we must realize how important it is to not just listen mindlessly, but to let the other person know that we are making the effort to clarify and understand how they feel. This does not mean that we cannot disagree with them; we can, and should, let them know what points we disagree on and try to come to a compromise. But we must see their side too, and be sympathetic. This creates good will, openness to change, and compromise on both sides.

Freud encouraged the patient to think about himself. Understanding oneself is like turning the light on in a dark room filled with unknown demons. Intelligent introspection is a great therapeutic instrument.

When facing a difficult conflict in our families, we can benefit from this principle. If we learn how to look inside ourselves, into our motives and feelings, we can begin to see the situation more clearly. We become more able to listen objectively to the other person once we've learned to listen to ourselves.

He was never punitive toward the patient for being sick. Before Freud, most therapies for mental illness involved some form of punishment: isolation, bleeding, chains, or dunking into ice water. Most nonprofessional listeners become angry after a few hours if the supplicant "doesn't listen" or "refuses" to get better. Freud tried to learn to restrict his anger and frustration, but imposed no such limitations on the patient. He respected his patients, cared for them, treated them with dignity. They were important to him, and he hoped that they would learn to become important to themselves.

In a similar way, we can try not to react in unreasonable, punitive ways to what others are telling us when we disagree with their views or feelings about things. We need to respect other family members' individuality and right to their own opinions and needs. In this way we can avoid conflict and keep both sides open to honest compromise.

Freud established the precedent that the therapist should have an erudite mind, be a scholar. The psychoanalyst should study history, literature, anthropology, mythology, and other disciplines, and try to apply this knowledge to helping the patient. Freud imagined himself to be like an archaeologist, an explorer of the patient's past, and encouraged other therapists to follow his example.

Sometimes it's helpful for us to understand the social or cultural causes for the conflicts we are facing within our families. For example, the women in the family, especially the mother, can feel unjustly burdened with most of the responsibility, if not all, for caring for the house and children, while often also having a job outside the home. This is not just a problem with her husband as an individual. It is a societal problem: cultural and social beliefs most of us have absorbed throughout our formative years have taught us that certain roles are "manly" and certain roles are "feminine." Perhaps nobody—family or teachers—ever taught us much about shared responsibilities and the equality of men and women so widely accepted today.

Freud kept all information confidential. He never reported his findings to the patient's family, the police, or religious authorities, or used confidential information for his personal gain.

We can apply this practice to our own relationships today as well. When we brag or tell about something confidential that was told to us by a family member or friend, we automatically anger and betray that person and, more importantly, jeopardize our relationship by violating their trust in us.

Freud recognized the limitations of his technique. He constantly reminded himself as well as others that psychoanalysis was not a panacea, that some day chemists might supply the ultimate answers.

We too should accept and recognize our own limitations: as parents, children, wives, siblings, friends. None of us is perfect, and through an ongoing drive toward self-improvement we can greatly increase our chances of having healthy relationships with others.

He allowed a patient his freedom. The patient was a free agent, could terminate his treatment at will, and owed his doctor no permanent loyalty. He was free to express his anger, disappointment, and passions without fear of retaliation. Freud never tried to manage a patient's life; it was the patient's responsibility to learn to manage his own life. He tried to help his patients to think constructively, but refused to become a manager of reality. He never established a cult following among his patients, and his followers were physicians who were free to leave his scientific discipline (and many did).

We, too, need to learn how to allow others, no matter how close to us they may be, to follow their own paths, choose their own ways of living their lives, and make their own decisions. Just as we would like to be free to feel and act as we desire, we must give others the same privilege.

SERMONETTE

Sigmund Freud genuinely tried to help his patients. He was a dedicated physician. Stripped of the metapsychology, his techniques are as valid today as when he first developed them. He was the first therapist to establish person-to-person therapy; no amount of today's available biological-chemical treatments can replace personal involvement. This was the genius of Freud, and not his theories of behavior, which were always subject to change. No priest, no medicine man, no religious leader ever conceived of such an approach as the solution to many of our emotional problems. Yet skilled practitioners of this personal approach are still in short supply. Theories may change, but the basics remain the same, even today. Freud's work is the solid foundation of all of the variations of psychotherapy today.

Perhaps adult children, their elderly parents, and the family as a whole can learn to live with and respect one another if they try to communicate and to understand what they are feeling. It doesn't really matter if their understanding is perfect; it's more important that they are interested and trying.

For these insights, I would like to express my appreciation and tribute to Sigmund Freud.